Beta Mathematics 1

New Edition

Compiled by

T. R. Goddard

J. W. Adams and R. P. Beaumont

 Schofield & Sims Ltd Huddersfield

0 7217 2258 X

First printed 1979
Reprinted 1979 (twice)
Reprinted 1980 (twice)
Reprinted 1982
Revised and reprinted 1984
Reprinted 1985
Reprinted 1987
Reprinted 1989
Revised and reprinted 1992
Reprinted 1994

The books in the two series forming this programme comprise:

Ready for Alpha and Beta 0 7217 2266 0

Beta Mathematics 1 0 7217 2258 X	Alpha Mathematics 1 0 7217 2250 4
Beta Mathematics 2 0 7217 2259 8	Alpha Mathematics 2 0 7217 2251 2
Beta Mathematics 3 0 7217 2260 1	Alpha Mathematics 3 0 7217 2252 0
Beta Mathematics 4 0 7217 2261 X	Alpha Mathematics 4 0 7217 2253 9

Printed in England by Chorley & Pickersgill Ltd, Leeds

Contents

Beta Mathematics 1

Counting to 10

0	nought; zero
● 1	one
● ● 2	two
● ● ● 3	three
● ● ● ● 4	four
● ● ● ● ● 5	five
● ● ● ● ● ● 6	six
● ● ● ● ● ● ● 7	seven
● ● ● ● ● ● ● ● 8	eight
● ● ● ● ● ● ● ● ● 9	nine
● ● ● ● ● ● ● ● ● ● 10	ten

A

1 Count the number of counters in each row.

2 Learn to spell the number words.

3 Count on from 0 to 10 to your partner.

4 Count back from 10 to 0 to your partner.

5 Begin at 3. Count on to 7.
   Write and complete: 3, □, □, □, 7.

6 Begin at 9. Count back to 2.
   Write and complete: 9, □, □, □, □, □, □, 2.

B

Draw these cards. Write as a word, the number of dots on each.

1 2 3 4 5 6

How many in each set below? Write the number as a figure.

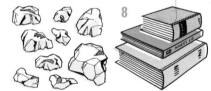  

7 8 9 10 11

12 Write the number words for 6, 3, 9, 5, 10.

13 Write figures for two, seven, one, four, zero, eight.

C

Copy this list. Count and then write the number in each set as a figure and as a number word.

set of	number	number word
Stars		
Balls		
Dolls		
Kites		
Rings		

Signs
= + −

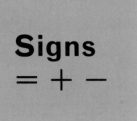

A

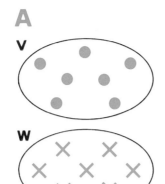

Count the number of dots in set **V**.

Count the number of crosses in set **W**.

The number of dots **is the same as** the number of crosses.

The number of crosses **is equal to** the number of dots.

$$7=7$$

> **The sign = means 'is the same as'**
> **'is equal to'.**

1 Which set **X**, **Y** or **Z** has nine members?

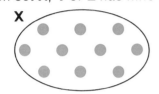  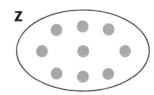

2 Which sets have an equal number of members? Draw them and put the sign = between them.

B

1 Count the number of pennies.

2 How many more pennies must be added to 4p to make 6p?

3 Write and fill in the missing numbers.
$4+\square=6$ $\square+4=6$

> **The plus sign + means 'add'.**

4 How many more pennies must be added to 4p to make 9p?

5 Write and fill in the missing numbers.
$4+\square=9$ $\square+4=9$

Write and fill in the missing numbers.

6 $5+\square=7$
$\square+5=7$

7 $6+\square=6$
$\square+6=6$

8 $7+\square=9$
$\square+7=9$

9 $3+\square=8$
$\square+3=8$

C

1 Count the number of apples.

2 How many apples are taken away to leave 5?

3 Write and fill in the $\square$.
$7-\square=5$

> **The minus sign − means 'take away'**
> **or 'subtract'.**

4 How many apples are taken from 7 to leave 4?

5 Write and fill in the $\square$.
$7-\square=4$

Write and fill in the missing numbers.

6 $8-5=\square$
$8-\square=5$

7 $6-\square=6$
$6-\square=0$

8 $7-6=\square$
$7-\square=6$

9 $9-\square=7$
$9-\square=2$

6

Addition to **10**

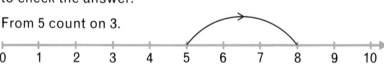

A

1 By counting, find
how many pennies in pile **M**. 5 pennies.
How many pennies in pile **N**? 3 pennies.

2 How many pennies are there
altogether? Count them.

3 Look at this number line
to check the answer.

From 5 count on 3.

$$0\quad 1\quad 2\quad 3\quad 4\quad 5\quad 6\quad 7\quad 8\quad 9\quad 10$$

Write and fill in the □.

4 5 add □=8　　5 □+3=8　　6 5 plus 3=□　　7 □+5=8
8 How many more than 5 is 8?　　9 How many more than 3 is 8?

B

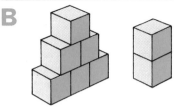

1 By counting, find
how many bricks in each pile.
How many bricks are there altogether?

2 Draw a number line and show that
$6+2=8$　　$2+6=8$.

Write and fill in the □.

3 □ add 2 equals 8.　　4 The total of 6 and 2 is □.　　5 6 plus □=8
6 The sum of 6 and 2 is □.　　7 8 is □ more than 2.　　8 8 is □ more than 6.

C Use a number line to find the answers.

1 2+2=□　　5 4 add 3=□　　9 8 add 2=□　　13 Find the total of
2 1 add 9=□　　6 1 plus 6=□　　10 9+0=□　　　　0 and 5.
3 5 add 4=□　　7 3+7=□　　11 1 add 8=□　　14 Find the sum of
4 10 plus 0=□　　8 2 add 4=□　　12 5 plus 5=□　　　3 and 6.

D Write these answers in figures and in words.

1 Five more than nought
2 The total of three and four
3 Nought add eight
4 Three plus two
5 Six more than four
6 The sum of six and one
7 Four add four
8 Five plus two
9 Two more than seven
10 Three plus three plus three

E **Number stories**

1 Jack spends 2p and then 5p. How much has he spent altogether?

2 Jane is 7 years old and David is 2 years older. How old is David?

3 Mother gave Tim 6 sweets and then 3 more. How many sweets has he?

4 The sum of two equal numbers is 6. Find the numbers.

5 Make up four **addition** number stories. The answers should be 10 or less.

Subtraction to 10

A

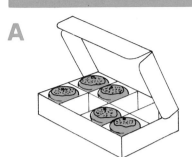

1 By counting, find
how many cakes the box holds when full. 8 cakes.
How many cakes have been taken away? 3 cakes.

2 How many cakes are left? Count them.

3 Look at this number line to check the answer.

From 8 count back 3

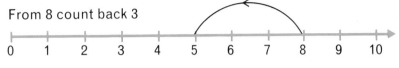

Write and fill in the ☐.

4 8 take away 3 leaves ☐.

7 8 minus 3 equals ☐.

5 ☐ subtract 3 equals 5.

8 8−3=☐

6 5 is ☐ less than 8.

9 3 is ☐ less than 8.

B

There are 9 blue counters.

There are 4 white counters.

1 What is the difference between 9 and 4?
Write and complete: 9−4=☐.

2 What is the difference between 9 and 5?
Write and complete: 9−5=☐.

Find the difference between

3 6 and 1

4 7 and 10

5 8 and 2

6 1 and 9.

7 Find two numbers less than 5 which have
a difference of 3.

8 Find two numbers less than 7 which have
a difference of 5.

C

Use the number line to find the answers if
you wish.

1 7 take away 2=☐

2 6 subtract 4=☐

3 8 take away 0=☐

4 9 subtract 7=☐

5 6 minus 2=☐

6 6 less than 10=☐

7 8 minus 4=☐

8 Take 2 from 4=☐.

9 10−4=☐

10 3−0=☐

11 7−6=☐

12 9−9=☐

Find the difference between

13 4 and 3

14 10 and 5

15 7 and 3

16 9 and 2

17 2 and 5

18 0 and 7

19 3 and 10

20 4 and 9.

D

Number Stories

1 By how many pennies is 6 pennies less
than 9 pennies?

2 Tom had 8 marbles. He lost 6. How many
had he left?

3 Tim is 7 years old. Joan is 5 years younger.
How old is Joan?

4 Richard has 6 sweets. Susan has 3 less.
How many sweets has Susan?

5 Jack is 10 years old. Tom is 2. What is
the difference in their ages?

6 Mother bought 7 stamps. She used 4 of
them. How many stamps had she left?

7 Alan had 9 nuts. He gave away 3. How
many had he left?

8 Make up four **subtraction** number
stories using 10 as the biggest number.

Addition and subtraction to 10

A Write and complete.

1

$3+4=\square$
$4+\square=7$
$7-3=\square$
$7-\square=3$

Notice that only three numbers 7, 3 and 4 are used in the examples in the box.

2

8

5   3

$5+3=\square$
$3+\square=8$
$8-5=\square$
$8-\square=5$

3

9

5   4

$5+4=\square$
$4+\square=9$
$9-5=\square$
$9-\square=5$

In this way write four number facts for 10 using: **4** 7 and 3   **5** 8 and 2   **6** 4 and 6.

B Write the answers only.

1	$(2+4)+1$	**7**	$(5+3)-1$	**13**	$\begin{array}{r}2\\3\\+4\\\hline\end{array}$	**15**	$\begin{array}{r}0\\7\\+3\\\hline\end{array}$	**17** $(8-2)-1$

1 $(2+4)+1$
2 $(5+0)+2$
3 $(3+4)+3$

4 $(6+3)+0$
5 $(1+7)+2$
6 $(0+0)+8$

7 $(5+3)-1$
8 $(7+2)-3$
9 $(8+1)-5$

10 $(2+6)-3$
11 $(5+4)-8$
12 $(6+3)-3$

13 $\begin{array}{r}2\\3\\+4\\\hline\end{array}$

14 $\begin{array}{r}1\\6\\+3\\\hline\end{array}$

15 $\begin{array}{r}0\\7\\+3\\\hline\end{array}$

16 $\begin{array}{r}0\\0\\+9\\\hline\end{array}$

17 $(8-2)-1$
18 $(10-6)-2$
19 $(9-2)-7$

20 $5-(3+1)$
21 $7-(2+2)$
22 $10-(5+3)$

C

Write each of the following without words using numbers and the signs $=$, $+$, $-$ only.

1 Six plus three equals nine.
2 Seven taken from ten leaves three.
3 Eight minus three equals five.
4 The sum of two and seven equals nine.
5 One subtract nought equals one.

6 The difference between eight and six equals two.
7 Ten take away five leaves five.
8 Six plus two minus seven equals one.
9 The difference between nought and four equals four.
10 The total of three, two and four equals nine.

D

The sign $<$ means 'is less than'.

9, 4, 7, 10, 2   Which of these numbers are less than 6?
Write: $4<6$; $2<6$.

Use the sign $<$ to write:
1 5 is less than 8
4 6 is less than 7

2 7 is less than 10
5 $(3+4)$ is less than 9

3 0 is less than 1
6 $(7-2)$ is less than 8.

The sign $>$ means 'is greater than'.

10, 6, 3, 8, 5   Which of these numbers are greater than 7?
Write: $10>7$; $8>7$.

Use the sign $>$ to write:
7 1 is greater than 0
10 7 is greater than 6

8 5 is greater than 2
11 $(6-1)$ is greater than 3

9 8 is greater than 5
12 $(8+2)$ is greater than 9.

Write the missing sign $=$, $<$ or $>$ in place of $\bullet$.
13 $4+4 \bullet 8$
16 $10-5 \bullet 1+6$

14 $7 \bullet 2+3$
17 $8-7 \bullet 0+1$

15 $4+2 \bullet 2+4$
18 $5+2 \bullet 7-0$

Money to 10p   coins

A Get one of each of the coins shown in the picture.

A 10p coin is called a TEN.
A 5p coin is called a FIVE.
A 2p coin is called a TWO.
A 1p coin is called a penny.

1 What is the shape of each coin?
The coins are either silver or copper (bronze) in colour.

2 Name
a the silver coins   b the copper coins.
Feel round the edge of each coin.

3 Which coins have
a a smooth edge   b a rough or milled edge?

4 Which of these coins has
a the greatest value   b the least value?

5 Write and complete:
1 TEN = ☐ FIVES   1 TEN = ☐ TWOS.

B Find the total value of the coins in each box.

1

2

3

4

5

6

7

8

9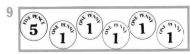

C Write the value of the missing coin or coins in each box.

1

5（2）+〇+（2）+〇+（1）=9p

2 （2）+（5）+〇=9p

6 （5）+〇=10p

3 （2）+〇+（2）+（2）=8p

7 （2）+〇+（2）+（2）+〇=10p

4 （5）+（2）+（2）+〇=10p

8 （5）+（1）+〇+〇+〇=10p

Money to 10p

coins

A **David buys an article for 8p.**
He can pay for it in different ways.

Price
8p

8 pennies or
4 TWOS or
1 FIVE and 3 pennies or
1 FIVE, 1 TWO and 1 penny

1 Write the way in which David uses
a the least number of coins
b the greatest number of coins.

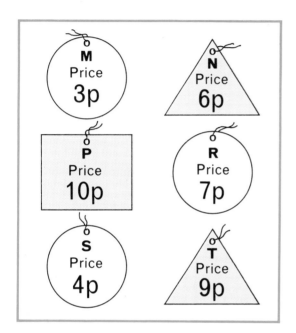

M Price **3p**

N Price **6p**

P Price **10p**

R Price **7p**

S Price **4p**

T Price **9p**

These drawings are price labels taken
from different articles. Draw the table
below.

Write the coins which pay each price.

Use the least number of coins.

The first is done for you.

	price	coins used
2	3p	2p+1p
3	6p	
4	10p	
5	7p	
6	4p	
7	9p	

Each price label is given a letter
M, N, P, R, S, T.

Find the total cost of

8 articles **M** and **R**   9 articles **N** and **S**   10 articles **M** and **S**   11 articles **M** and **N**.

B How much change is given from a TEN
after paying for one article costing

1 7p   2 10p   3 8p

4 9p   5 4p   6 1p

7 6p   8 2p   9 3p?

10 John gave a TEN to pay for articles
costing 4p and 5p. How much change
did he receive?

11 Mary bought an ice cream costing 6p.
She had 3p left. How much had she at
first?

12 How many 2p balloons can be bought
for a TEN?

13 Richard buys 3 choc-bars costing 3p
each. He receives 1p change. Name the
coin he gave to pay for them.

Find the difference in price between

14 7p and 2p   15 4p and 9p

16 3p and 8p   17 5p and 10p.

18 Tom has 1 FIVE and 2 TWOS in his
pocket. He spends 6p. How much has
he left?

Counting to 20

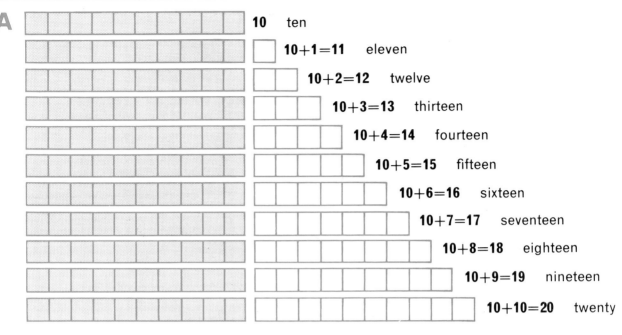

A

10	ten	
	10+1=11	eleven
	10+2=12	twelve
	10+3=13	thirteen
	10+4=14	fourteen
	10+5=15	fifteen
	10+6=16	sixteen
	10+7=17	seventeen
	10+8=18	eighteen
	10+9=19	nineteen
	10+10=20	twenty

1

T	U
1	7

Draw the columns and write in these numbers. The first is done for you.

seventeen	fifteen
nine	nineteen
eleven	twelve
thirteen	sixteen
eighteen	ten
twenty	fourteen

Write these numbers in words.

2 1 ten and 3 units   7 1 ten and 2 units
3 1 ten and 1 unit   8 1 ten and 9 units
4 1 ten and 7 units   9 1 ten and 4 units
5 1 ten and 5 units   10 2 tens and 0 units
6 1 ten and 8 units

B Write the answers only.

1 10+4   5 3+10   9 18−10   13 12−2
2 10+6   6 5+10   10 11−10   14 19−9
3 10+0   7 2+10   11 13−10   15 14−4
4 10+10   8 9+10   12 17−10   16 10−0

C Write the following using the signs +, −, = only and then find the answers.

> **Example: 1 more than 10**   1+10=11

1 1 less than 11   5 13 take away 3.   9 The difference between 17 and 7
2 Add 10 to 5.   6 10 more than 10   10 The sum of 10 and 9
3 16 minus 10   7 Take 6 from 16.   11 10 less than 20
4 10 plus 2   8 The total of 4 and 10   12 The difference between 8 and 18

Counting to 20

A

0 1 2 3 4 5 6 7 8 9 10 11 12 13 14 15 16 17 18 19 20

Write the missing numbers.

1 From 7 count on to 11.   7, ☐, ☐, ☐, 11
2 From 9 count on to 16.   9, ☐, ☐, ☐, ☐, ☐, ☐, 16
3 From 17 count back to 9.   17, ☐, ☐, ☐, ☐, ☐, ☐, ☐, 9
4 From 11 count back to 6.   11, ☐, ☐, ☐, ☐, 6

5 $7+☐=17$
6 $9+☐=16$
7 $17-☐=9$
8 $11-☐=6$

Write the answers only. Use the number line if you wish.

9
3+ 2
13+ 2
3+12

10
5+ 4
15+ 4
5+14

11
9+ 1
19+ 1
9+11

12
0+ 7
10+ 7
0+17

13
2+ 6
12+ 6
2+16

14
7− 2
17− 2
17−12

15
8− 3
18− 3
18−13

16
10− 7
20− 7
20−17

17
5− 4
15− 4
15−14

18
9− 0
19− 0
19−10

Write the answers only.

B
1 11+ 3
2 13+ 5
3 2+16
4 4+12
5 17+ 3
6 4+14
7 15+ 5
8 18+ 2
9 5+12
10 14+ 6
11 7+11
12 12+ 6
13 4+15
14 11+ 5
15 3+14

C
1 0+18
2 2+15
3 12+ 3
4 7+13
5 11+ 8
6 16+ 4
7 13+ 6
8 11+ 9
9 6+11
10 8+12
11 13+ 4
12 12+ 7
13 14+ 5
14 16+ 3
15 15+ 3

D
1 15− 3
2 17− 2
3 14− 4
4 18− 5
5 12− 1
6 16− 0
7 19− 6
8 13− 2
9 17− 5
10 15− 1
11 13− 0
12 18− 3
13 16− 4
14 15− 3
15 19− 4

E
1 19−17
2 14−12
3 11− 1
4 15− 4
5 14− 2
6 19− 5
7 18− 7
8 16− 5
9 18−14
10 15− 5
11 19−12
12 18− 6
13 19− 8
14 15−12
15 17−14

F Copy and put in the missing sign
+, − or = in place of the ●.

1 2 ● 13=15
2 13 ● 11=2
3 14+5 ● 19
4 15+3 ● 12+6
5 19−3 ● 10+6
6 8 ● 11=20 ● 1

G Copy and put in the missing sign
=, > or < in place of the ●.

1 11 ● 7+14
2 16 ● 9+10
3 8+4 ● 16−4
4 12−8 ● 9+4
5 17−5 ● 14−3
6 8+7 ● 0+15

Number order first, second, third ......

A The scores of the children playing a game are:

name	Peter	Ann	Tom	Sally	Alan	Jane
score	15	12	7	18	10	9

1 How many children played the game?
2 Name the child who had
   a the highest score   b the lowest score.
3 Write the scores in order putting the highest score first.
4 Write the scores in order putting the highest score last.

5

| 4p | 20p | 13p | 16p | 2p | 11p | 8p | 15p |

Which of these amounts of money is
a the greatest   b the smallest?
c Write the amounts in order putting the greatest first.
d Of this order, which is the last but one?

B

ball   car   skittle   engine   doll   clock   chair   bottle   ruler   box

1 Count how many articles there are in the row.
2 Name the article which is
   a first   b last   c last but one in the row.
3 The car is second in the row.
   Name the article which is
   a third   b fourth   c fifth in the row.
4 What is the order in the row of
   a the clock   b the ruler   c the box?
5 Name the article which is
   a the seventh   b the eighth in the row.

6 Make a list of the articles in order.

ball	first
car	second
skittle	third

Write by the side of each the word which tells its place in the row.

C Which letter in the word **MATHEMATICS** is
1 second; third; fourth; eighth;   2 1st; 5th; 9th; 10th?
3 S is the last letter. Write its number order as a word; as a symbol.

A B C D E F G H I J K L M N O P Q R S T

These are the first 20 letters of the alphabet in order. Write the letter which is

4 seventh; thirteenth; eighteenth; twentieth;
5 2nd; 7th; 11th; 16th.
6 This is the thirteenth page in this book. What is the heading on the 18th page?

Money   counting coins to 20p

A

1   John has these coins in his pocket.
Write and complete : John has ☐ TEN and ☐ pennies.   John has ☐p altogether.

In the boxes there are the coins which Mary, Philip, Joan and Tom have in their pockets.

MARY   PHILIP

JOAN   TOM

	TEN	pennies
John	1	4
Mary		
Philip		
Joan		
Tom		

2   Copy this table. Write in the amount of money each child has.

3   Write these amounts in words.

4   Mary changes some of her pennies. She then has a TEN and 3 coins. Name them.

5   Change the pennies of the other children for a smaller number of coins.

6   Write and complete: a Philip has ☐p less than Mary.
                          b Joan has ☐p more than John.

7   How much more than Tom has   a John   b Mary   c Philip   d Joan?

8   How much more must each child save to have 2 TENS?

9   Write the children's money in order, putting the smallest first.

B   How much money is there in each of these boxes?

1      3      5

2      4      6

Check the answers.

7   How much more is needed to make each up to 20p? Write the six answers in the same order.

Money addition and subtraction to 20p

A 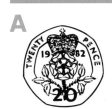 The picture shows a 20p coin, called a TWENTY.

1 What is its colour, silver or copper? 2 Has it a smooth or a milled edge?

3 The shape of a TWENTY is **not** a circle. It has curved sides. How many?

4 Write and complete:

1 TWENTY = ☐ TENS   1 TWENTY = ☐ FIVES   1 TWENTY = ☐ TWOS.

Four children had these coins in their pockets.

Susan	5 5 5
Joy	2 2 2 2 2
Roger	10 5 2 1
Tim	5 5 1 2 1 2

5 How much money had
   a Susan   b Joy   c Roger   d Tim?

6 How much less than a TWENTY had
   a Susan   b Joy   c Roger   d Tim?

7 What is the difference between the largest and smallest amounts?

8 Susan, Joy, Roger and Tim each spent 7p. How much had each child left?

B

1 Write the name of each child. Then find how much money each child has left after going shopping.

2 Work with a partner and make up more examples like these.

name	coins in purse				money spent	money left
Mary	5	2	2	2	7p	
Joan	10	5	2	1	9p	
Tony	5	5	5	1	8p	
Alan	10	2	2		6p	
Ann	5	2	2	10	12p	

C Find the value of the missing coins in each box.

1  5 + 2 + ◯ + ◯ = 9p

2 5 + 5 + ◯ + ◯ = 14p

3 10 + 2 + ◯ + ◯ = 15p

4 Draw the table. Write the coins which make up these prices. **Use the least number of coins.**

prices	coins used
13p	10p + 2p + 1p
17p	
15p	
18p	
19p	
14p	

Addition and subtraction facts to 18

A Look at the number line.

1

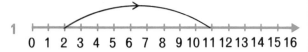

From 2 count on 9.
From 9 count on 2.
Write and complete: 2 and 9 equals ☐
9 plus 2 equals ☐.

2

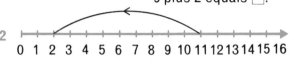

From 11 count back 9.
From 11 count back 2.
Write and complete:
11 take away 9 equals ☐
11 minus 2 equals ☐.

3 You see that there are three numbers
11, 2 and 9 about which two addition
and two subtraction facts are written.
Write and complete.

11
2   9

2+9=☐   11−9=☐
9+2=☐   11−2=☐

4 Using 11, 3 and 8 write and complete
these number facts. Look at the number
line again if you wish.

11
3   8

3+8=☐   11−8=☐
8+3=☐   11−3=☐

5 In the same way, write and complete
these number facts.

11
4   7

4+7=☐   11−7=☐
7+4=☐   11−4=☐

11
5   6

5+6=☐   11−6=☐
6+5=☐   11−5=☐

B Write and complete these number facts
for 12. Use a number line if you wish.

1

12
3   9

3+9=☐   12−9=☐
9+3=☐   12−3=☐

2

12
4   8

4+8=☐   12−8=☐
8+4=☐   12−4=☐

3

12
5   7

5+7=☐   12−7=☐
7+5=☐   12−5=☐

4

12
6   6

6+6=☐   12−6=☐

C Write the answers only.
1 From 12 take away 5.
2 Find the total of 6 and 5.
3 Take 7 from 11.
4 Find the difference between 6 and 12.
5 How many more than 2 is 11?
6 How many less than 12 is 4?
7 11 minus 8
8 What must be added to 8 to make 12?
9 Find the total of 2, 6 and 3.
10 From 11 take the sum of 7 and 2.

D Find the missing number.
1 4+☐=11   6 2+☐=11
2 12−☐=3   7 ☐−8=4
3 ☐+9=12   8 ☐−6=5
4 ☐+5=11   9 4+☐+2=12
5 12−7=☐   10 3+8−☐=5

Addition and subtraction facts to 18

A

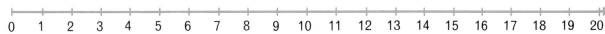

Write and complete these number facts for 13. Use the number line if you wish.

Write in the same way, the number facts for each of the following.

1

13
4   9

4+9=☐   13−9=☐
9+4=☐   13−4=☐

2

13
5   8

5+8=☐   13−8=☐
8+5=☐   13−5=☐

3

13
6   7

6+7=☐   13−7=☐
7+6=☐   13−6=☐

4

14
5   9

5

14
6   8

6

14
7   7

7

15
6   9

8

15
7   8

9

16
7   9

10

16
8   8

11

17
8   9

12

18
9   9

B Write the answers only.

1 How many more than 8 is 16?
2 9 plus 8
3 14 minus 6
4 Find the total of 8 and 3.
5 Take 7 from 14.
6 What must be added to 4 to make 13?

7 From 15 take 9.
8 By how many is 8 less than 15?
9 Find the difference between 7 and 15.
10 What is the sum of 6, 2 and 7?
11 From 13 take the sum of 4 and 5.
12 Add 8 to the difference between 4 and 11.

C Find the missing numbers.

1 5+☐=13
2 14−☐=9
3 ☐+7=16
4 18−9=☐
5 9+☐=17
6 ☐−6=9

7 8+☐=13
8 ☐−7=8
9 8+☐=14
10 ☐−7=6
11 6+☐+4=15
12 9+7−☐=10

13 7+☐=13
14 17−9=☐
15 ☐+7=15
16 ☐−9=7
17 5+☐=12
18 14−☐=6

19 8+☐=17
20 ☐−6=7
21 ☐+7=12
22 12−☐=8
23 8+2+☐=16
24 4+6−☐=3

D Write the answers only. First add upwards.   Check the answer by adding downwards.

1
```
  3
  4
+ 7
___
```

2
```
  5
  8
+ 5
___
```

3
```
  7
  2
+ 9
___
```

4
```
  6
  5
+ 7
___
```

5
```
  9
  0
+ 6
___
```

6
```
  8
  7
+ 3
___
```

Measuring length
paces, foot-lengths

Pacing

John is finding the length of the class-room. He is pacing the distance. You can do this, too.

1 Stand with your back to the wall.

2 Walk forward, counting the paces.

3 Write and complete:
The class-room is ☐ paces long.
Its length is ☐ paces.

4 In the same way, count the paces to find the width of the room. Write and complete:
The class-room is ☐ paces wide.
Its width is ☐ paces.

5 On squared paper draw a picture of the class-room floor. The picture is called a **plan.** Put in the length and width in paces.

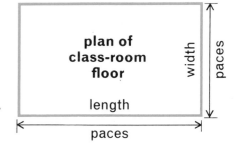

plan of class-room floor

length

width

paces

paces

Heel to toe

Mary is finding the length and width of the room by walking heel to toe and counting by foot-lengths.

6 Find the length and width of the class-room floor in foot-lengths.

7 Draw another plan and put in the measurements in foot-lengths.

B

distance		in paces	in foot-lengths
class-room	length		
	width		
hall	length		
	width		
corridor	length		

1 Copy this table and enter the measurements.

2 Measure a in paces, b in foot-lengths, the school hall, other rooms, a corridor.

3 Why is the number of paces always less than the number of foot-lengths?

4 Why is it quicker to measure the school hall by pacing than by foot-lengths?

5 Look at the measurements found by other boys and girls. If they differ from yours, can you say why this is?

Measuring length   spans

A

Spanning

Place your hand on the desk.

Open your fingers wide.

The distance between the thumb and the little finger is called a **span**.

Tom is using his span to measure the length of the top of his desk.

Use your span to find these distances and then write and complete:

1 The top of the desk is ☐ spans long.
   Its length is ☐ spans.

2 The top of the desk is ☐ spans wide.
   Its width is ☐ spans.

3 The desk is ☐ spans high.
   Its height is ☐ spans.

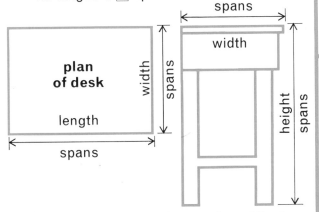

4 On squared paper, draw a plan of the top of the desk.
   Put in the length and width in spans.

5 Make a drawing on squared paper of your desk and put in its height and width in spans.

B

measure		in spans
desk	length	
	width	
	height	
table	length	
	width	
	height	
cupboard	length	
	width	
	height	

1 Copy this table and fill in the span measurements.

2 Measure the length, width and height of other things in spans, e.g. tables, cupboards, etc.

3 Compare each set of measurements with those made by other children. If they are different, say why.

4 Why would you not measure the length and width of a room in spans?

C Many years ago people measured lengths and distances in paces, foot-lengths or spans.

Cloth was measured from the tip of the nose to the end of the fingers of the outstretched arm.

You have found out that body measurements can vary, they can be long or short according to the size of the person.

A fixed or **standard measure, which is always the same,** is now used.

Measures length

metres
m

A The standard measure of length is called a **metre (m)**.

1 Get a metre stick. Place it on the floor along the edge of the wall. Mark lengths of 1 metre; 2 metres; 3 metres.

2 Is the length of your pace longer or shorter than 1 metre?

3 Place the metre stick upright against the wall. Mark heights of 1 metre; 2 metres.

4 Is your own height greater or less than 1 metre; greater or less than 2 metres?

5 From a piece of string cut off a length of 1 metre. Use it to find
   a three articles each longer than 1 metre
   b three articles each shorter than 1 metre.

	estimate metres	measure metres	estimate correct too long too short
class-room length width			
school hall length width			

B 1 Copy this list.

2 Estimate (guess) the length and width of the class-room in metres. Write them in the table.

3 Now measure both distances in metres. Measure in a straight line along the edge of the floor.

4 Estimate (guess) and measure in metres, other lengths and widths. Write them in the list. Were your estimates correct or too long or too short?

5 Compare your measurements with other children's. They should be the same. Why?

centimetres
cm

C When measuring there may be a length left over which is too small to measure with a metre stick. Therefore, a smaller measure is made by dividing the metre into 100 equal parts.

Each part is called a **centimetre (cm)**.

The picture shows a ruler marked in centimetres.

Find the length of each object in cm.

Counting in tens to 100

A

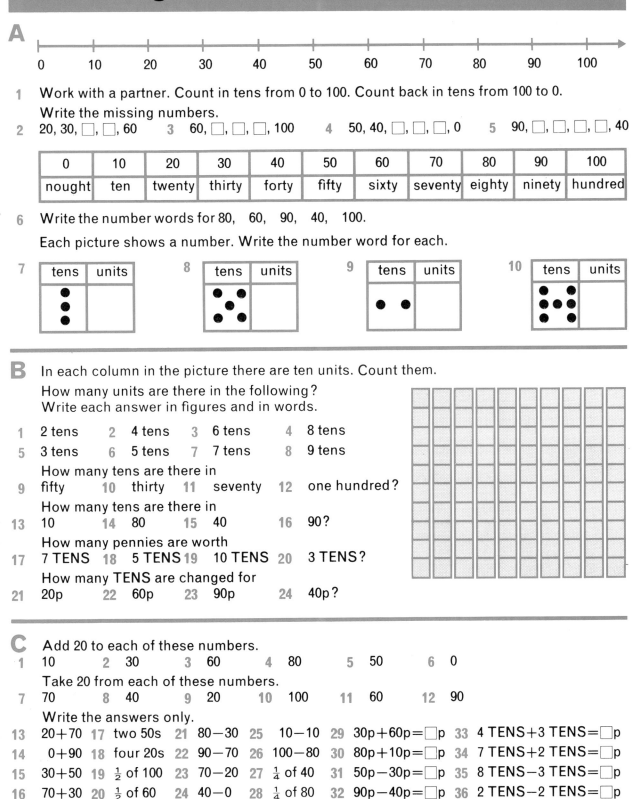

0   10   20   30   40   50   60   70   80   90   100

1   Work with a partner. Count in tens from 0 to 100. Count back in tens from 100 to 0.

Write the missing numbers.

2   20, 30, ☐, ☐, 60   3   60, ☐, ☐, ☐, 100   4   50, 40, ☐, ☐, ☐, 0   5   90, ☐, ☐, ☐, ☐, 40

0	10	20	30	40	50	60	70	80	90	100
nought	ten	twenty	thirty	forty	fifty	sixty	seventy	eighty	ninety	hundred

6   Write the number words for 80,   60,   90,   40,   100.

Each picture shows a number. Write the number word for each.

7

tens	units

8

tens	units

9

tens	units

10

tens	units

B   In each column in the picture there are ten units. Count them.

How many units are there in the following?
Write each answer in figures and in words.

1   2 tens   2   4 tens   3   6 tens   4   8 tens
5   3 tens   6   5 tens   7   7 tens   8   9 tens

How many tens are there in

9   fifty   10   thirty   11   seventy   12   one hundred?

How many tens are there in

13   10   14   80   15   40   16   90?

How many pennies are worth

17   7 TENS   18   5 TENS   19   10 TENS   20   3 TENS?

How many TENS are changed for

21   20p   22   60p   23   90p   24   40p?

C   Add 20 to each of these numbers.

1   10   2   30   3   60   4   80   5   50   6   0

Take 20 from each of these numbers.

7   70   8   40   9   20   10   100   11   60   12   90

Write the answers only.

13   20+70   17   two 50s   21   80−30   25   10−10   29   30p+60p=☐p   33   4 TENS+3 TENS=☐p
14   0+90   18   four 20s   22   90−70   26   100−80   30   80p+10p=☐p   34   7 TENS+2 TENS=☐p
15   30+50   19   ½ of 100   23   70−20   27   ¼ of 40   31   50p−30p=☐p   35   8 TENS−3 TENS=☐p
16   70+30   20   ½ of 60   24   40−0   28   ¼ of 80   32   90p−40p=☐p   36   2 TENS−2 TENS=☐p

Tens and units

A

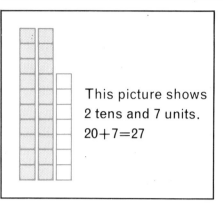

This picture shows
2 tens and 7 units.
20+7=27

Write in the same way the number each picture shows.

1
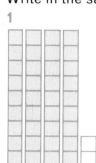

2
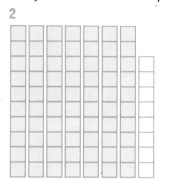

3
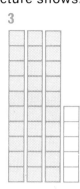

B

Write the number shown in each picture. The first one is done for you.

1
tens	units

4 tens 1 unit
40+1=41

2
tens	units

3
tens	units

4
tens	units

5
tens	units

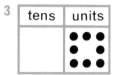
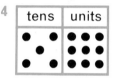
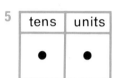

C

On these picture numbers each bead
stands for **one ten** (T) or **one unit** (U)
according to its place.

Write the number shown in each picture
as in **B1** above.

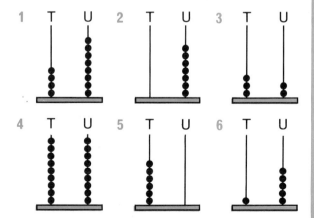

1 T U 2 T U 3 T U

4 T U 5 T U 6 T U

These pictures are taken from an **abacus**.
Find out about an abacus from a book
in the library.
You should make an abacus.

7 Draw abacus pictures to show these
numbers.
57, 80, 33, 4

D

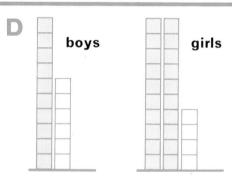

boys   girls

1 John counts the boys in his class and then
draws the picture to show the number.
How many boys were there in the class?

2 He then counts the girls and draws
another picture. How many girls?

3 How many children were there altogether
in the class?

4 Count the boys and girls in your class
and draw the picture numbers of each.

5 Count all the chairs in your class-room.
Draw a picture like those in **B** to show
the number.

6 How many pages are there in this book?
Draw an abacus picture to show the
number.

Tens and units

A

1 Draw the columns and write the numbers. The first two are done for you.

H	T	U	
		7	seven
	1	3	thirteen
			forty
			sixty-nine
			twenty-two
			fifty-one
			ninety
			10 tens

2 Write these as numbers.
6 tens and 3 units   3 tens and 4 units
1 ten and 9 units   7 tens and 0 units
5 units   9 tens and 6 units

3 What is the biggest number which can be written in
a the units column
b the tens column?

B

Write and fill in the missing numbers.

1 $15 = \square$ ten 5 units
2 $33 = 3$ tens $\square$ units
3 $67 = \square$ tens 7 units
4 $82 = 8$ tens $\square$ units
5 $50 = \square$ tens 0 units

6 $27 = \square$ tens $\square$ units
7 $58 = \square$ tens $\square$ units
8 $10+10+10+4 = \square$ tens $\square$ units $= \square$
9 $20+10+10+9 = \square$ tens $\square$ units $= \square$
10 $40+10+10+2 = \square$ tens $\square$ units $= \square$

C

Work with a partner taking turns.

1 Count on in tens from 4 to 94; 7 to 97.

2 Count back in tens from 95 to 5; 98 to 8.

3 Add 10 to each of these numbers.
5, 37, 90, 41

4 Take 10 from each of these numbers.
13, 42, 78, 100

Write the missing numbers in these series.

5 26, 36, $\square$, $\square$, 66
6 52, $\square$, $\square$, $\square$, 92
7 3, $\square$, 43, $\square$, 83
8 81, 71, $\square$, $\square$, 41
9 69, $\square$, $\square$, $\square$, 29
10 94, 74, $\square$, $\square$, 14

11 Read the numbers in the table. The 1 moves to the left. 0 fills the empty spaces.

12 What happens to the value of the 1 each time it is moved to the left?

H	T	U
		1
	1	0
1	0	0

D

Write the answers only.

1 $40+9$
2 $80+12$
3 $10+56$
4 $30+28$
5 $43+20$
6 $40+50+7$
7 $29-10$
8 $33-20$
9 $90-50$
10 $58-40$
11 $74-4$
12 $85-5-30$

E

Write the answers only.

1 3 more than 10
2 The total of 17 and 40
3 Take 4 from 60.
4 Add 11 to 70.
5 From 80 take 1.
6 The sum of 18 and 80
7 6 less than 50
8 25 plus 30

Find the difference between
9 60 and 6
10 3 and 90.

F

Write the answers only.

1 4 TENS + 7p
2 3 TENS + 16p
3 From 6 TENS take 8p.
4 Take 2p from 2 TENS.
5 14p more than 7 TENS
6 9p less than 5 TENS

How many to make up
7 23 to the next ten
8 55 to the next ten
9 34p to the next TEN
10 97p to the next TEN?

Whole ones, halves and quarters

A

1 whole apple   John shares it equally with Tom.   There are 2 equal parts.

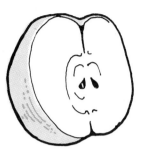

2 halves = 1 whole one

$$\frac{1}{2} + \frac{1}{2} = 1$$
$$\frac{2}{2} = 1$$

John has a
whole apple.

John has one half.
$$\frac{1}{2}$$

Tom has one half.
$$\frac{1}{2}$$

B

Mary shares it equally with Jane, Ann and Sally.

1 whole orange

Mary has a
whole orange.

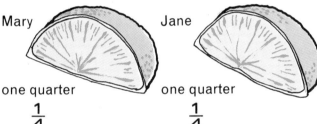

Mary   Jane

one quarter
$$\frac{1}{4}$$

one quarter
$$\frac{1}{4}$$

Mary and Jane together have one half. $\frac{2}{4} = \frac{1}{2}$

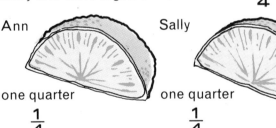

Ann   Sally

one quarter
$$\frac{1}{4}$$

one quarter
$$\frac{1}{4}$$

Ann and Sally together have one half. $\frac{2}{4} = \frac{1}{2}$

There are
4 equal parts.

$$\frac{4}{4} = 1$$

C

1   John cut his share of the apple into two
equal parts. Write the name of each part
in figures and in words.

2   Mary had put her quarter with Ann's
quarter. What part of the whole orange
do they make?

3   Tom eats one half of his piece of apple.
What part of the whole apple has he left?

4   Jane, Ann and Sally put their parts of the
orange together.
What part of the whole orange did they
make?

Whole ones, halves and quarters

A

1 Get a strip of paper. Fold it into 2 equal parts.
Mark each part $\frac{1}{2}$. Write: $\frac{1}{2}+\frac{1}{2}=1$.

$\frac{1}{2}$	$\frac{1}{2}$

2 Get another strip of paper. Fold it in half and then in half again. Into how many equal parts is the strip divided?
Mark each part $\frac{1}{4}$. Write: $\frac{1}{4}+\frac{1}{4}+\frac{1}{4}+\frac{1}{4}=1$.

3 Cut off $\frac{1}{4}$. What part of the strip is left?

4 Get a piece of string.
Fold and cut it into two halves.
Now, by folding and cutting, find $\frac{1}{4}$ of the piece of string.
Do this again with different lengths of string.

B

Here are six shapes all of which are called **squares.**

Each square is a **whole one** folded to show either halves or halves and quarters.

1   4

2   5

3   6

Write the part $\frac{1}{2}$, $\frac{1}{4}$ or $\frac{3}{4}$ of each square which is shaded.

C

whole one

$\frac{1}{2}$	$\frac{1}{2}$

1 This shape is called a **rectangle**.
It has been folded into 2 equal parts.
Each part is $\frac{1}{2}$.

Get three pieces of paper which are rectangles. Fold each piece, in a different way, into 2 equal parts.

Make a drawing of each to show the fold line. Mark each part $\frac{1}{2}$.

whole one

$\frac{1}{4}$	$\frac{1}{4}$	$\frac{1}{4}$	$\frac{1}{4}$

2 This rectangle has been folded into 4 equal parts. Each part is $\frac{1}{4}$.

Get two pieces of paper which are rectangles. Fold each piece, in a different way, into 4 equal parts.

Make a drawing of each rectangle to show the fold lines. Mark each part $\frac{1}{4}$.

D

This shape is called a **circle.**

1 Get three round tin lids of different sizes. Draw round the edge of each and then cut out the circles.
Each circle is a **whole one.**

2 Take one circle. Fold it into 2 equal parts. Shade $\frac{1}{2}$ of the circle.

3 Fold another circle into 4 equal parts. Name each part.

4 Fold another circle and cut out $\frac{3}{4}$ of it.

5 What part of the circle is left?

+ and − number facts to 10 to 18 practice tests

Put a strip of plain paper by the side of list **A** and write the answers.
Mark them and correct any mistakes.
Then go on to list **B** and do the same again.
In the same way work in turn tests **C** to **J**.

A		**B**		**C**		**D**		**E**	
1	1+9	1	7+2	1	2+8	1	3+4	1	8+2
2	3+7	2	3+6	2	9+0	2	8+1	2	6+1
3	5+0	3	4+4	3	5+2	3	6+3	3	7+0
4	6+4	4	2+4	4	3+3	4	5+5	4	1+9
5	3+2	5	0+8	5	4+5	5	4+1	5	2+3
6	5+4	6	4+6	6	7+3	6	6+2	6	4+2
7	4+3	7	3+5	7	2+6	7	2+7	7	6+4
8	2+5	8	1+7	8	1+5	8	0+6	8	5+3

F		**G**		**H**		**I**		**J**	
1	10−2	1	6−4	1	9−3	1	5−3	1	10−5
2	8−1	2	9−8	2	8−2	2	9−7	2	6−3
3	7−0	3	7−6	3	10−4	3	7−4	3	8−7
4	9−6	4	5−0	4	7−3	4	10−9	4	9−0
5	7−2	5	8−6	5	9−9	5	8−4	5	5−2
6	10−6	6	10−3	6	6−2	6	9−2	6	10−8
7	8−3	7	9−4	7	8−5	7	6−5	7	7−7
8	5−4	8	7−5	8	10−7	8	8−8	8	9−5

In the same way work in turn tests **K** to **T**. Use the number line if you wish.

0 1 2 3 4 5 6 7 8 9 10 11 12 13 14 15 16 17 18

K		**L**		**M**		**N**		**O**	
1	9+9	1	7+5	1	9+8	1	3+8	1	9+3
2	5+7	2	3+9	2	8+6	2	7+8	2	5+9
3	8+4	3	9+7	3	7+4	3	4+9	3	4+7
4	7+7	4	6+7	4	6+9	4	6+8	4	9+6
5	8+9	5	9+5	5	8+7	5	5+6	5	8+5
6	6+5	6	8+3	6	4+8	6	8+8	6	7+9
7	9+4	7	5+8	7	2+9	7	7+6	7	6+6

P		**Q**		**R**		**S**		**T**	
1	12−7	1	18−9	1	14−7	1	11−9	1	12−5
2	13−9	2	15−8	2	17−9	2	13−4	2	11−6
3	12−6	3	11−7	3	11−3	3	15−7	3	13−7
4	14−8	4	17−8	4	13−5	4	12−8	4	16−8
5	13−6	5	14−6	5	15−6	5	14−9	5	12−3
6	16−9	6	12−9	6	11−8	6	16−7	6	15−9
7	11−5	7	13−8	7	12−4	7	11−4	7	14−5

Practise these tests again and again.

Money using coins 20p, 10p, 5p, 2p, 1p

Complete these tables for change from 1 TEN and 1 TWENTY.
Write and learn them.

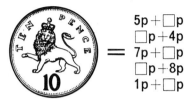
$$5p + \square p$$
$$\square p + 4p$$
$= \quad 7p + \square p$
$$\square p + 8p$$
$$1p + \square p$$

$$2p + \square p$$
$$\square p + 16p$$
$= \quad 1p + \square p$
$$\square p + 3p$$
$$10p + \square p$$

$$13p + \square p$$
$$\square p + 9p$$
$= \quad 15p + \square p$
$$\square p + 8p$$
$$14p + \square p$$

A Write the answers only.

1	10p − 5p	4	10p − 2p
2	10p − 3p	5	10p − 6p
3	10p − 9p	6	10p − 7p

7	20p − 11p	10	20p − 18p
8	20p − 17p	11	20p − 12p
9	20p − 6p	12	20p − 4p

B Write the answers only.

1 $15p = 11p + \square p$
2 $15p = \square p + 14p$
3 $15p = 3p + \square p$
4 $15p = \square p + 2p$

5 $15p − 12p = \square p$
6 $15p − 4p = \square p$
7 $15p − 13p = \square p$
8 $15p − 1p = \square p$

9 $20p = 19p + \square p$
10 $20p = 7p + \square p$
11 $20p = 5p + \square p$
12 $20p = 2p + \square p$

13 $20p − \square p = 4p$
14 $20p − \square p = 11p$
15 $20p − \square p = 6p$
16 $20p − \square p = 3p$

C

Find the total of
1 1 TEN and 3 TWOS
2 1 FIVE and 7 pennies
3 4 TWOS and 5 pennies
4 1 FIVE and 5 TWOS
5 1 TEN, 6 pennies and 2 TWOS
6 1 TEN, 1 FIVE, 1 TWO and 1 penny
7 2 TWOS, a FIVE and 9 pennies
8 3 FIVES and 4 pennies.

Find the missing number of coins.
9 16p = $\square$ TEN, $\square$ TWOS
10 11p = $\square$ FIVE, $\square$ TWOS
11 17p = $\square$ TEN, $\square$ FIVE, $\square$ TWO
12 19p = 7 pennies, $\square$ TWOS
13 9p = $\square$ FIVE, $\square$ TWOS
14 18p = 3 pennies, $\square$ FIVES
15 20p = 1 TEN, $\square$ TWOS
16 20p = 2 FIVES, 3 TWOS, $\square$ pennies

D Draw these tables, then fill them in. The first example in each table is done for you.

Which 2 coins together
make the given amount?

amount	2 coins
15p	10p + 5p
7p	
11p	
12p	
10p	
20p	
6p	
4p	

Which 3 coins together
make the given amount?

amount	3 coins
8p	5p + 2p + 1p
9p	
17p	
13p	
11p	
16p	
20p	
14p	

Which single coin is of
the nearest value to pay
these amounts?

amount	coin	change
3p	5p	2p
9p		
6p		
4p		
18p		
15p		
14p		

Numbers from pictures   weather-chart

A John and Mary made a weather-chart.
This is what they did.

1 They cut out some squares of gummed paper and drew
pictures on them to show a sunny day, a rainy day,
a dull day.

    sunny   **rainy**   **dull**

2 At 3.00 p.m. each day they agreed if the day had
been sunny, rainy or dull.

3 They stuck a picture square in its proper column on
the chart.

B

1 Count the number of sunny, rainy and dull days in the
weather-chart.

Draw and fill in this table.

weather	sunny	rainy	dull
number of days			

Answer these questions.

2 How many more sunny days were there than rainy days?

3 How many more sunny days were there than dull days?

4 There were twice as many sunny days as _____ days.

5 There were _____ as many dull days as sunny days.

6 On how many days altogether did John and Mary look
at the weather?

7 During which of these months do you think John and
Mary made the chart?

November   **January**   **June**

C Work with a partner and make a weather-record for
two weeks.

You can invent more and different kinds of picture
squares if you wish.

The weather-chart looked like this.

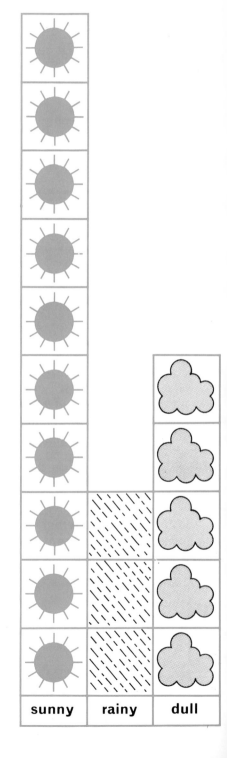

Numbers from pictures   graphs

A Susan made this picture graph to show the number of children who were absent each day from class.

1 On a sheet of squared paper she drew five rows, one for each day.

2 For each child who was absent for the whole day, a 'pin child' was drawn. The picture shows how the graph looked at the end of the week.

day	number of children absent
Monday	👤 👤 👤 👤 👤 👤 👤 👤
Tuesday	👤 👤 👤 👤 👤
Wednesday	👤 👤 👤
Thursday	👤 👤 👤 👤
Friday	👤 👤 👤 👤 👤 👤

3 Draw this table. By counting, find how many children were absent each day. Write the numbers in the table.

4 If there were 27 children in the class, find how many children were at school each day.

day	number of children	
	absent	present
Monday		
Tuesday		
Wednesday		
Thursday		
Friday		

B The next week Susan made another picture graph but instead of drawing 'pin children' she put a cross to stand for each absent child.

At the end of the week the graph looked like this.

1 Draw another table, the same as before.

2 Write in the table how many children were
  a absent each day   b present each day.

day	number of children absent
Monday	X X X X X X
Tuesday	X X X
Wednesday	X
Thursday	X X X X
Friday	X X X X X X X

C The next week Susan made another graph. Instead of a cross, she put a shaded square to stand for each absent child.

1 On a sheet of squared paper, draw the rows and name the days as in the examples above.

2 Make a graph from the numbers shown in this table by shading one square for each absent child.

3 Keep a record every day for a week of the number of children who are absent from your class for a whole day.
  Then in the same way, on squared paper, draw a graph to show the numbers.

4 Find how many children were present each day.

day	number of children absent
Monday	4
Tuesday	3
Wednesday	0
Thursday	2
Friday	7

Measures   length

A Get a ruler marked in
centimetres only.
Measure each of these lines.

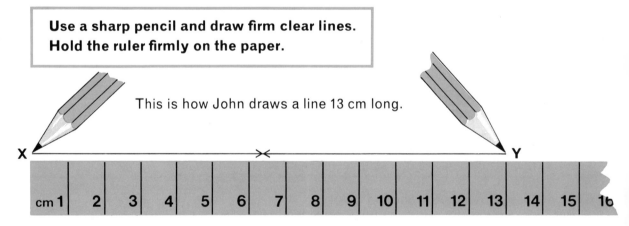

B Learn and practise how to draw lines exactly to given measurements.

> **Use a sharp pencil and draw firm clear lines.**
> **Hold the ruler firmly on the paper.**

This is how John draws a line 13 cm long.

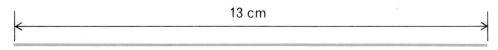

Put the pencil point, as shown, at mark **X** which is the beginning of the ruler.
Draw inwards for a short distance following the arrow.
Put the pencil point exactly on the 13 cm mark at **Y**.
Draw inwards again following the arrow until the line is complete.
Now write in the measurement like this.

13 cm

Draw lines of these lengths and write in the measurements.

5 cm   8 cm   11 cm   17 cm   14 cm   20 cm

Measures length   estimating and measuring

A

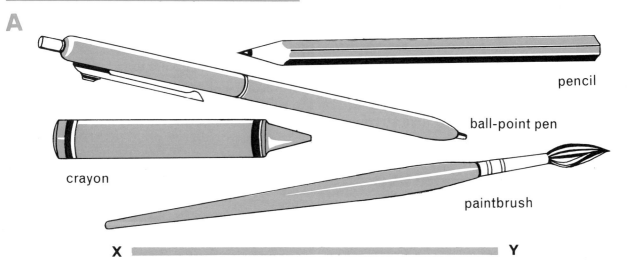

pencil

ball-point pen

crayon

paintbrush

X ———————————————————— Y

1 Look at each of the pictures.
Make a list of the things in order of length
writing the shortest first.
Do not measure them.

2 Estimate (guess) which of the things are
a shorter than the line **XY**
b longer than the line **XY**
c the same length as the line **XY**.

3 Measure the length of the line. Put away
your ruler.

4 Now estimate (guess) the length in cm of
a the ball-point pen   c the pencil
b the paintbrush   d the crayon.

5 Measure each one in cm. Find out and
write whether your estimates were
correct, too long or too short.

B   You are going to do more estimating and measuring in centimetres only.

1 Copy this table.

2 Estimate the length of your
longest finger.

3 Now measure it. Find whether your
estimate is correct, too long or
too short.

4 Do the same again with the book;
the desk.
Keep a record of your results.

5 Make another list of 6 objects which
are less than 1 metre long,
e.g. pictures, boxes, books, etc.

6 Estimate and measure their lengths
in cm.

7 Find in each case if your estimate
was correct, too long or too short.

8 Keep a record of your work.

		estimate cm	measure cm	estimate correct too long too short
longest finger				
book	length width			
desk	length width height			

You will notice that when measuring these things
there is usually a small length left over which is
too small to measure in centimetres.
Find out how a smaller measure has been made
for this purpose.

Telling the time

A Look at the clock face.

The **hour-hand** (the small one) points to 3.
The **minute-hand** (the large one) points to 12.

1 Write: The time is ☐ o'clock or 3.00.

In the same way, write the time shown on each of these clocks.

2   **3**   **4**   **5**   **6**

Clock 6 shows 12 o'clock which in daytime is called **midday** or **noon** and at night is called **midnight**.

Times between **midnight** and **midday** are shown as **a.m.**

Times between **midday** and **midnight** are shown as **p.m.**

7 Write the morning time for clock 2; clock 4.

8 Write the afternoon time for clock 3; clock 5.

B   **Time to ½ hour; ¼ hour** | **1 hour (h) = 60 minutes (min)**

1 Write $\frac{1}{2}$ h = ☐ min; $\frac{1}{4}$ h = ☐ min; $\frac{3}{4}$ h = ☐ min.

a    **b**    **c**    **d**    **e**

quarter past 1   half past 1   quarter to 2
1.15   1.30   1.45

f    **g**    **h**    **i**    **j**

The times on clocks **a**, **b**, and **c** are written in two ways.

2 Write in two ways the time on each of the clocks **d, e, f, g, h, i** and **j**.

3 Write in figures the morning times for clocks **d, f, h** and **j**.

4 Write in figures the afternoon times for clocks **e, g** and **i**.

C   Write these times in figures. Use a.m. or p.m.

1   10 o'clock at night   2   one hour before midday   3   quarter to 12 in the morning

4   4 o'clock in the morning   5   quarter past 8 in the evening   6   half an hour before midday

7   one hour after midnight   8   half past 11 at night   9   one hour before midnight

Telling the time to 5 minutes

Look at the clock face.
The **hours** are numbered 1, 2, 3, 4 . . . to 12.
The **minutes** are marked between the **hour numbers**.

A By counting, find how many **minutes** between the **hour numbers**

1 12 and 1　　　2 7 and 8　　　3 2 and 4　　　4 7 and 9

5 3 and 6　　　6 9 and 12　　　7 12 and 4　　　8 6 and 11.

To tell the time to 5 minutes

Count the minutes past the hour
to 30 min (the half hour).

Count the minutes to the next hour
after the half hour (30 min).

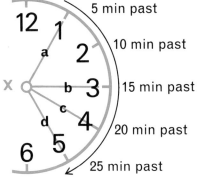

Practise counting on:
5 10 15 20 25 30

Practise counting back:
30 25 20 15 10 5

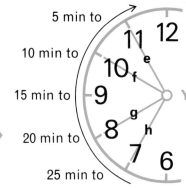

9 Look at the half-clock **X**.

How many minutes **past the hour** is it for
each of the hands marked **a, b, c** and **d**?

10 Look at the half-clock **Y**.

How many minutes **to the next hour** is it
for each of the hands marked **e, f, g** and **h**?

B

5 min past 1
1.05

1 Write in two ways the time on each of the clocks **b, c, d, e**.

5 min to 1
12.55

2 Write in two ways the time on each of the clocks **g, h, i, j**.

3 Write in figures the morning times for clocks **a, c, e, g, i**.

4 Write in figures the afternoon times for clocks **b, d, f, h, j**.

Counting in twos

A

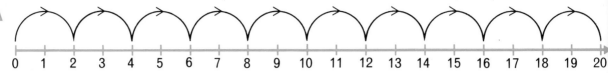

| 0 | 1 | 2 | 3 | 4 | 5 | 6 | 7 | 8 | 9 | 10 | 11 | 12 | 13 | 14 | 15 | 16 | 17 | 18 | 19 | 20 |

Look at the number line.   Count on in **twos** from 0 to 20.   Count back in **twos** from 20 to 0

Complete these series.

1   6, 8, ☐, ☐, 14, 16, ☐, 20

2   20, 18, ☐, ☐, 12, 10, ☐, ☐, ☐, 2, ☐

3   1, 3, ☐, 7, 9, ☐, ☐, ☐, 17, ☐

4   19, 17, ☐, ☐, 11, ☐, 7, ☐, 3, ☐

B

There are 2 wheels on the bicycle.

1   On 4 bicycles there are $2+2+2+2=$☐ wheels.

There are 4 sets each of 2 wheels.

Instead of **adding equal sets** you can **multiply**.

> **The sign $\times$ means multiply by or times.**

2   How many wheels are
there on 4 bicycles?
Write in full:
4 twos = 4(2) = ☐
4 multiplied by 2=☐
4 times 2=☐
$4\times2=$☐.

3   How many wheels are
there on 7 bicycles?
Write in full:
$2+2+2+2+2+2+2=$☐
7 twos = 7(2) = ☐
7 multiplied by 2=☐
7 times 2=☐
$7\times2=$☐.

4   How many wheels are there
on 10 bicycles?
Write:
10 twos = 10(2) = $10\times2=$☐.

5   How many wheels are there
on 0 bicycles?
Write:
0 twos = 0(2) = $0\times2=$☐.

C   3 sets of 2

1   3 twos = 3(2) = $3\times2=$☐

2 sets of 3

2   2 threes = 2(3) = $2\times3=$☐

> $6 = 3\times2 = 2\times3$
> 6 is the **product** of
> 2 and 3.

Write and complete:

3   $8 = 4\times2 = 2\times$☐

4   $12 = 6\times2 = 2\times$☐

5   ☐ $= 1\times2 = 2\times$☐

6   $10 = 5\times$☐ $=$ ☐$\times5$

7   $16 = 8(2) = 2($☐$)$

8   $14 = 7(2) =$ ☐(7).

Find the product of

9   2 and 10

10   6 and 2

11   2 and 8

12   4 and 2

13   2 and 1

14   2 and 5

15   0 and 2

16   2 and 9

17   2 and 2

18   2 and 7.

Counting in twos

A

1 By counting in **twos** find how many pennies.

   Write and complete: $5 \times 2p = \square p$.

2 How many sets of 2 are there in 10?

3 Share 10 pennies equally between 2 boys. How many pennies for each boy?

4 This can be written in two ways.

   Write and complete:

   $10p \div 2 = \square p$ $2)\overline{10p}^{\;\square p}$.

The sign ÷ means divide by or share.

---

5 How many FIVES have the same value as 10 pennies?

6 Share 10 pennies equally among 5 boys. How many pennies for each boy?

7 This can be written in two ways.

   Write and complete:

   $10p \div 5 = \square p$ $5)\overline{10p}^{\;\square p}$.

   Write and complete:

8 $8 \div 2 = \square$ $8 \div 4 = \square$

9 $14 \div 2 = \square$ $14 \div 7 = \square$

10 $20 \div 2 = \square$ $20 \div 10 = \square$

11 $16 \div 2 = \square$ $16 \div 8 = \square$.

B Write and complete:

1 $\begin{array}{|c|}\hline \;^{\quad 2}\\ 10 \\ _5 \quad \\\hline\end{array}$
   $5 \times 2 = \square$
   $2 \times 5 = \square$
   $10 \div 2 = \square$
   $10 \div 5 = \square$

2 $\begin{array}{|c|}\hline \;^{\quad 2}\\ 18 \\ _9 \quad \\\hline\end{array}$
   $9 \times 2 = \square$
   $2 \times 9 = \square$
   $18 \div 2 = \square$
   $18 \div 9 = \square$

3 $\begin{array}{|c|}\hline \;^{\quad 2}\\ 6 \\ _3 \quad \\\hline\end{array}$
   $3 \times 2 = \square$
   $2 \times 3 = \square$
   $6 \div 2 = \square$
   $6 \div 3 = \square$

4 $\begin{array}{|c|}\hline \;^{\quad 2}\\ 12 \\ _6 \quad \\\hline\end{array}$
   $6 \times 2 = \square$
   $2 \times 6 = \square$
   $12 \div 2 = \square$
   $12 \div 6 = \square$

5 $\begin{array}{|c|}\hline \;^{\quad 2}\\ 16 \\ _8 \quad \\\hline\end{array}$
   $8 \times 2 = \square$
   $2 \times 8 = \square$
   $16 \div 2 = \square$
   $16 \div 8 = \square$.

6 In the same way, write four facts about each of these numbers.

   8   2   20   14

C

1 In the shortest way, find the total of $2+2+2+2+2+2$.

2 What number is twice 8?

3 To double a number multiply it by 2. Double these numbers.

   2   4   7   9   1

4 A pair or couple is two. How many are 8 pairs; 3 couples; 5 pairs?

5 How many pairs in 12;   18?

6 Find one half of 14;   2;   20.

7 Divide 20 by 2.

8 How many times can 2 be taken from 16?

9 Share 18p equally between John and Joan. How much each?

   Write and complete:

10 $\square \times 2 = 2$

11 $0 \div 2 = \square$

12 $\square \times 10 = 20$.

Counting in twos

A Copy and complete the **tables of twos**.

Table of twos ✗	Table of twos ÷
0 × 2 = ☐	0 ÷ 2 = ☐
☐ × 2 = 2	☐ ÷ 2 = 1
2 × ☐ = 4	4 ÷ ☐ = 2
3 × 2 = ☐	6 ÷ 2 = ☐
☐ × 2 = 8	☐ ÷ 2 = 4
5 × ☐ = 10	10 ÷ ☐ = 5
6 × 2 = ☐	12 ÷ 2 = ☐
☐ × 2 = 14	☐ ÷ 2 = 7
8 × ☐ = 16	16 ÷ ☐ = 8
9 × 2 = ☐	☐ ÷ 2 = 9
☐ × 2 = 20	☐ ÷ 2 = 10

Check both tables and make sure they are correct.

Write the answers only.
Look carefully at the signs × or ÷.

1 3 × 2
2 10 ÷ 2
3 6 × 2
4 14 ÷ 2
5 1 × 2
6 0 ÷ 2
7 9 × 2
8 4 ÷ 2

9 0 × 2
10 6 ÷ 2
11 2 × 2
12 2 × 7
13 8 ÷ 2
14 2 × 4
15 16 ÷ 2
16 2 × 5

17 12 ÷ 2
18 2 × 8
19 20 ÷ 2
20 2 ÷ 2
21 2 × 10
22 18 ÷ 2

Mark the answers and correct any mistakes in full.

B

1	②	3	④	5	6	7	8	9	10
11	12	13	14	15	16	17	18	19	20

1 Copy the chart on squared paper.

2 From 2 count on in twos and put a ring round the numbers.

3 Write the ringed numbers.
2, 4, ☐, ☐, ☐, ☐, ☐, ☐, ☐, ☐
Check if each number divides exactly by 2.
These are called **even** numbers.

4 Write in order the numbers which are not ringed. 1, 3, ☐, ☐, ☐, ☐, ☐, ☐, ☐, ☐
Check that each number does not divide exactly by 2.
These are called **odd** numbers.

5 Which of these numbers are even?
8   11   2   10   17   20   14   9

6 Which of these numbers are odd?
17   18   4   9   16   3   19   1

7 To each of these odd numbers, add 1.

3	7	13	5	9	15

Are the answers odd or even numbers?

8 From each of the above odd numbers, subtract 1.
Are the answers odd or even numbers?

C Write the answers only.

1 (5 × 2) + 1
2 (2 × 9) + 1
3 (7 × 2) + 1
4 (0 × 2) + 1
5 6(2) + 1
6 1(2) + 1

7 10(2) + 1
8 8(2) + 1
9 15 ÷ 2 = ☐ rem. ☐
10 3 ÷ 2 = ☐ rem. ☐
11 21 ÷ 2 = ☐ rem. ☐
12 17 ÷ 2 = ☐ rem. ☐

13 John shares 16 sweets equally with his brother. How many sweets does each have?

14 Mother buys half a dozen eggs. How many eggs is that?

15 How many TWOS have the same value as a TWENTY?

16 What is the next even number after 28?

17 What is the next odd number after 19?

Measuring mass

A **You will need**

a large stone   a box of stones   a thick book
a brick   a wooden block   a bean bag.

1 Take the brick in one hand and the stone in the other as Tom is doing in the picture.

You are feeling the **mass** of the brick and the stone.

| lighter | heavier |

Choose the right word and write and complete:
The brick is _____ than the stone.
The stone is _____ than the brick.

2 Now take in your hands and feel the mass of the box of stones and the wooden block.
Write and complete:
The _____ is heavier than the _____ .
The _____ is lighter than the _____ .

3 In the same way, feel the mass of the book and the bean bag. Which is the heavier?

4 Choose other pairs of things. Feel the mass of each and then write which is the heavier.

> Notice that the word 'mass' is used instead of 'weight'.
> 'Weight' now means something different about which you will learn later.

B **Get a pair of scales.**

First make sure that one side balances the other.

1 Put the brick on one side of the scales and the stone on the other.

Which is the heavier, the brick or the stone?

Which is the lighter, the brick or the stone?

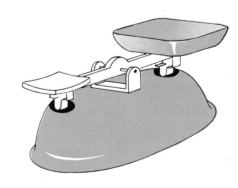

2 How do you know? Write a sentence.

3 In the same way, using the scales, find which is the heavier and which is the lighter:
a the box of stones or the wooden block
b the book or the bean bag.

Look again at your answers to questions **A1, 2** and **3** above and see if your estimates were correct.

4 By using the scales, check your answers to question **A4** above.

Measuring mass

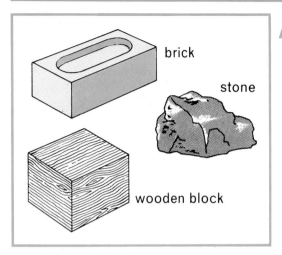

brick

stone

wooden block

A 1 Get the brick, the stone and the wooden block.
Feel in your hand the mass of each in turn.
Which do you estimate is the heaviest,
the lightest?
Write the objects in order, the lightest first.

2 Use only the scales for balancing to find which
is the heavier
a the brick or the stone
b the stone or the wooden block
c the brick or the wooden block.

3 Now write the objects in order, the lightest first.

4 Does this order agree with your estimate?

B Copy the record chart.

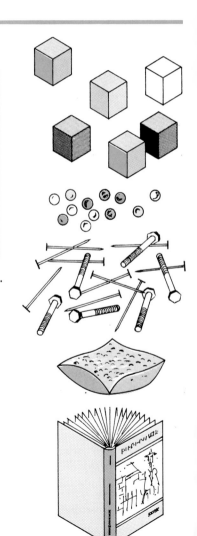

	number of		
	marbles	**wood cubes**	**iron bolts or large nails**
the stone wooden block bean bag book			

1 Use the scales to find how many marbles will balance the stone.
Write the number in the table.

2 Do the same for the other three things on the list.

3 Now weigh the four things again but this time use wood cubes
instead of marbles. Write the numbers in the table.

4 Look at the numbers. Choose the right word and write:

The number of marbles is always $\frac{\text{greater}}{\text{smaller}}$ than the number of
wood cubes.

Write a sentence giving the reason for this statement.

5 Weigh the four things again using iron bolts or large nails.
Count the number needed to balance each of the things.

6 Is the number of iron bolts or large nails greater than the
number of
a marbles   b cubes?

Measures mass

A

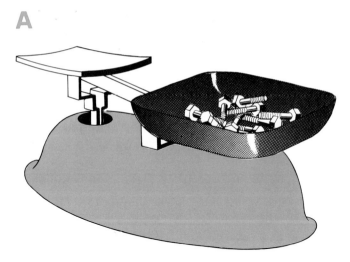

1 kilogram

½ kilogram

On the previous page, you discovered that when the mass of each of the things given in the list was measured first in marbles, then in cubes and in iron bolts or large nails a different answer was obtained for each.
This result tells you that **a measure, which is always the same,** is needed.

> The standard unit for measuring mass is the **kilogram (kg).**

In shops, fruit and vegetables, meat, packets of food, etc. are also sold by the **half-kilogram (½ kg).**

1 Get the scales and the 1 kg and ½ kg masses.
  Feel each mass in turn in your hand.

2 How many masses of ½ kg will balance 1 kg

3 Put the 1 kg mass on the scale pan and weigh
  a 1 kg of sand   b 1 kg of stones
  c 1 kg of iron bolts or large nails.
  Put each of them in a separate bag. Feel the mass of each. The mass of each is the same. Look at the quantity in each bag. What do you notice?

4 Weigh ½ kg of
  a large nails   b marbles   c conkers.
  Count the number of each.

5 Which is the heaviest; 1 nail, 1 marble or 1 conker?
  Write a sentence telling how you know.

B

1 Copy this record chart.

object	estimated mass
brick	more than ½ kg
stone	
box of sawdust	
box of pebbles	
bean bag	
wooden block	
milk bottle	

2 Collect all the things given in the list and some others.

3 Feel each one in your hand and estimate
  which has a mass of ½ kg,
  more than ½ kg or less than ½ kg.

  Write your estimates in the chart. The first has been done for you.

4 Use the scales and the ½ kg mass to check each estimate.

5 Find five objects in the class-room each of which you estimate has a mass of 1 kg. Use the scales and the 1 kg mass to find which are more or less than 1 kg.

Money   coins to £1

A

The picture shows a 50p coin called a FIFTY.

Make sure you can recognise it.
Get a FIFTY.

1 What is its colour, silver or copper?

2 Has it a smooth or a milled edge?

3 The shape of a FIFTY is **not** a circle. It has curved sides. How many?

4 Make a list of five things which cost about 50p each.

B

The picture shows a £1 coin.

Find from a £1 coin

1 its shape   2 its colour

3 its design.

4 Feel round the edge of the coin. What do you find?

5 Write and complete:
£1 = ☐ FIFTIES   £$\frac{1}{2}$ = ☐ pence.

6 Make a list of five things which cost about £1 each.

7 Notes (paper money) are used for larger numbers of £s. Find out their values.

C

How many TENS can be changed for
1 1 TWENTY   2 1 FIFTY   3 £1?

How many FIVES can be changed for
4 1 TEN   5 1 TWENTY
6 1 FIFTY   7 £1?

How many TWOS can be changed for
8 1 TEN   9 1 TWENTY
10 1 FIFTY   11 £1?

12 Write and complete these money tables.

£1 =
☐ 50p coins (FIFTIES)
☐ 20p coins (TWENTIES)
☐ 10p coins (TENS)
☐ 5p coins (FIVES)
☐ 2p coins (TWOS)
☐ 1p coins

1 FIFTY =
☐ 10p coins
☐ 5p coins
☐ 2p coins
☐ 1p coins

1 TWENTY =
☐ 10p coins
☐ 5p coins
☐ 2p coins
☐ 1p coins

1 TEN =
☐ 5p coins
☐ 2p coins
☐ 1p coins

D

£1 is worth:

1 1 FIFTY and ☐ TENS

2 1 FIFTY and ☐ FIVES

3 1 FIFTY, 1 TWENTY and ☐ FIVES

4 2 TWENTIES, 4 TENS and ☐ TWOS

5 3 TWENTIES, 3 TENS and ☐ pennies.

6 70p = 1 FIFTY and ☐ TWENTY

7 90p = 1 FIFTY and ☐ TWENTIES

8 65p = 1 FIFTY ☐ TEN and ☐ FIVE

9 65p = 1 FIFTY and ☐ FIVES

10 56p = 1 FIFTY and ☐ TWOS

Counting money to £1

A 1 **These are the coins in a money-box.**

Find the total value of the coins.
Count and then write the missing numbers.

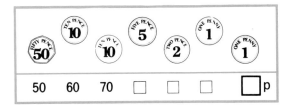

| 50 | 60 | 70 | ☐ | ☐ | ☐ | ☐p |

In the same way, find the total value of the coins in these boxes.

2

| 50 | 70 | ☐ | ☐ | ☐p |

3
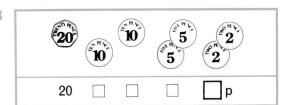

| 20 | ☐ | ☐ | ☐ | ☐p |

Now find the total value of the coins in each of these boxes.

4
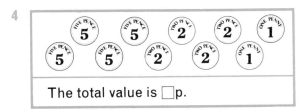

The total value is ☐p.

5
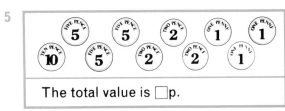

The total value is ☐p.

6
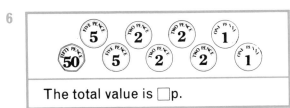

The total value is ☐p.

7
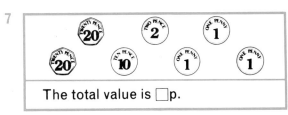

The total value is ☐p.

B John empties his money-box.
He sorts the coins into separate piles.

1 Copy this chart.

20p	10p	5p	2p	1p

2 Count and fill in the number of coins in each pile.

3 Find the total value of the coins.

Practise counting packets of money which your teacher gives you.

Lines and edges vertical, horizontal

A

Tim has tied a weight to a piece of string.

He is holding the string so that it hangs down.

Try this for yourself.

The string makes a straight line which hangs up and down. It is called a plumb line.

It is an **upright** line.

The **upright** lines shown are called **vertical** lines.

On squared paper draw three vertical lines measuring 3 cm, 5 cm, 8 cm.

Upright or vertical lines

B

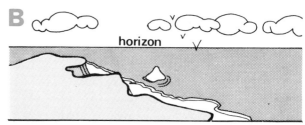

horizon

Tom looked out to sea. Where he saw the sea and the sky seem to meet is called the **horizon.** The horizon looks like a flat or level straight line.

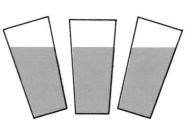

Get a glass half-filled with water. Tip the glass in different ways. What do you notice about the level of the water each time?

The level lines shown below are called **horizontal lines.**

Level or horizontal lines

On squared paper draw three horizontal lines measuring 4 cm, 2 cm, 7 cm.

C

The box is shown standing on a flat, horizontal table-top.

On squared paper draw the front of the box. It measures 8 cm long and 5 cm high.

Draw the vertical edges black, the horizontal edges red.

Front

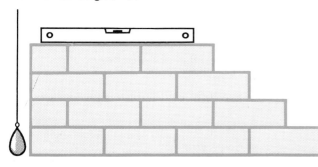

To build a wall the bricklayer uses a plumb line to build the edge of the wall vertically, and a spirit-level to lay the bricks in horizontal rows.

Make a plumb line like Tim's.

Ask your teacher how to make a spirit-level using a bottle filled with water.

Practise using both tools by testing vertical and horizontal edges in the class-room.

Lines and edges

vertical, horizontal, sloping

A

Some straight lines or edges are neither **vertical** nor **horizontal.**

They are **slanting** or **sloping** straight lines like these.

Draw five lines sloping
in different directions
measuring 3 cm, 6 cm, 9 cm, 2 cm, 8 cm.

B Use your ruler to measure in **centimetres**

1 the vertical lines. Write the letter of each and its length.
2 the horizontal lines. Write the letter of each and its length.
3 the sloping lines. Write the letter of each and its length.

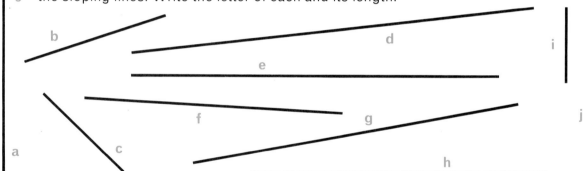

b   d   i

e

a   c   f   g   j

h

C On squared paper, draw these pictures the same size.

Colour the vertical lines and edges black,
        the horizontal lines and edges red,
        the sloping lines and edges green.

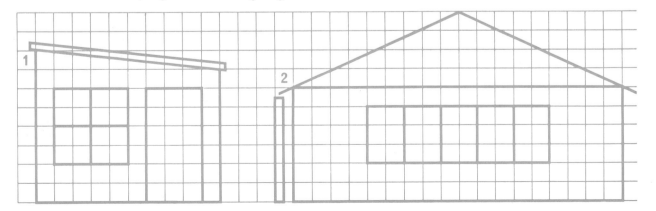

1

2

Counting in threes

A

1	2	③	4	5	⑥	7	8	⑨	10
11	12	13	14	15	16	17	18	19	20
21	22	23	24	25	26	27	28	29	30

1 Copy the chart on squared paper. From 3 count on in **threes** and ring the numbers.

2 Write the ringed numbers.
3, 6, ☐, ☐, ☐, ☐, ☐, ☐, ☐, 30

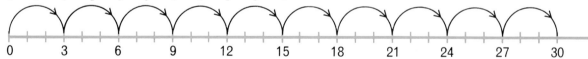

Copy and complete:

3 0, 3, 6, ☐, ☐, 15, ☐, 21

4 24, 21, ☐, ☐, ☐, 9, ☐, ☐, ☐

5 8, 11, ☐, ☐, 20, ☐, ☐, 29

6 22, 19, ☐, ☐, ☐, 7, ☐, ☐.

B

There are 3 wheels on the tricycle.

1 On 4 tricycles there are 3+3+3+3=☐ wheels.

There are 4 sets each of 3 wheels.

> **Remember** Instead of **adding equal sets** you can **multiply.**

2 How many wheels are there on 4 tricycles?
Write in full:
4 threes = 4(3) = ☐
4 multiplied by 3=☐
4 times 3=☐
4×3=☐.

3 How many wheels are there on 7 tricycles?
Write in full:
3+3+3+3+3+3+3=☐
7 threes = 7(3) = ☐
7 multiplied by 3=☐
7 times 3=☐
7×3=☐.

4 How many wheels are there on 8 tricycles?
Write: 8 threes = 8(3) = 8×3 = ☐.

5 How many wheels are there on 0 tricycles?
Write: 0 threes = 0(3) = 0×3 = ☐.

6 How many wheels are there on 10 tricycles?
Write:
10 threes = 10(3) = 10×3 = ☐.

Use the number line if you wish.

C

5 sets of 3

1 5 threes = 5(3) = 5×3 = ☐

> 15 = 5×3 = 3×5
>
> 15 is the **product** of 3 and 5.

3 sets of 5

2 3 fives = 3(5) = 3×5 = ☐

Write and complete:

3 3 = 1×3 = ☐×1

4 12 = 4×3 = 3×☐

5 21 = 7×3 = 3×☐

6 18 = 6×☐ = ☐×6

7 27 = 9(3) = 3(☐)

8 30 = 10(☐) = 3(☐).

Find the product of

9 3 and 6

10 3 and 4

11 7 and 3

12 3 and 10

13 1 and 3

14 8 and 3

15 3 and 3

16 3 and 0

17 9 and 3.

Counting in threes

A

1 By counting in **threes** find how many pennies.
Write and complete: $5 \times 3p = \square p$.

2 How many sets of 3 are there in 15?

3 Share 15 pennies equally among 3 boys. How many pennies for each boy?

4 This can be written in two ways. Write and complete:

$15p \div 3 = \square p \qquad 3)\overline{15p}^{\square p}$.

5 How many FIVES have the same value as 15p?

6 Share 15p equally among 5 boys. How many pennies for each boy?

7 This can be written in two ways. Write and complete:

$15p \div 5 = \square p \qquad 5)\overline{15p}^{\square p}$.

Write and complete:

8 $18 \div 3 = \square \qquad 18 \div 6 = \square$

9 $27 \div 3 = \square \qquad 27 \div 9 = \square$

10 $21 \div 3 = \square \qquad 21 \div 7 = \square$.

B

Write and complete:

1 | 12 | (3, 4) |
$4 \times 3 = \square$
$3 \times 4 = \square$
$12 \div 3 = \square$
$12 \div 4 = \square$

2 | 18 | (3, 6) |
$6 \times 3 = \square$
$3 \times 6 = \square$
$18 \div 3 = \square$
$18 \div 6 = \square$

3 | 27 | (3, 9) |
$9 \times 3 = \square$
$3 \times 9 = \square$
$27 \div 3 = \square$
$27 \div 9 = \square$

4 | 15 | (3, 5) |
$5 \times 3 = \square$
$3 \times 5 = \square$
$15 \div 3 = \square$
$15 \div 5 = \square$

5 | 21 | (3, 7) |
$7 \times 3 = \square$
$3 \times 7 = \square$
$21 \div 3 = \square$
$21 \div 7 = \square$.

6 In the same way, write four facts about each of these numbers. 6, 30, 24, 3

C

1 In the shortest way, find the total of
 a $3+3+3+3+3+3$
 b $3+3+3+3+3+3+3+3$.

2 9 multiplied by 3

3 Divide 21 by 3.

4 How many times can 3 be taken from 9?

5 What is the difference between 7 times 3 and 3 times 7?

6 In a bag are 3 apples. How many apples are there in 8 bags?

7 A pencil costs 3p. How many can be bought for 12p?

8 Share 18p equally among Tim, Joan and Jane. How much each?

9 30 cm of ribbon is divided into 3 equal pieces. What is the length of each piece?

10 1 TEN and 1 FIVE are shared equally among 3 children. How much did each receive?

Write and complete:

11 $\square \times 3 = 3$

12 $24 \div \square = 3$

13 $0 \div 3 = \square$

14 $10 \times \square = 30$

15 $\square \times 5 = 15$.

Counting in threes

A Copy and complete the **tables of threes**.

Table of threes ×	Table of threes ÷
0 × 3 = ☐	0 ÷ 3 = ☐
☐ × 3 = 3	☐ ÷ 3 = 1
2 × 3 = ☐	6 ÷ ☐ = 2
3 × 3 = ☐	9 ÷ 3 = ☐
☐ × 3 = 12	☐ ÷ 3 = 4
5 × 3 = ☐	15 ÷ ☐ = 5
☐ × 3 = 18	18 ÷ 3 = ☐
7 × 3 = ☐	☐ ÷ 3 = 7
☐ × 3 = 24	24 ÷ ☐ = 8
9 × 3 = ☐	☐ ÷ 3 = 9
☐ × 3 = 30	☐ ÷ 3 = 10

Check both tables and make sure they are correct.

Write the answers only.
Look carefully at the signs × or ÷.

1	1 × 3	9	9 × 3	17	3 × 10
2	0 ÷ 3	10	2 × 3	18	9 ÷ 3
3	3 × 3	11	12 ÷ 3	19	3 × 0
4	15 ÷ 3	12	3 ÷ 3	20	6 ÷ 3
5	6 × 3	13	3 × 5	21	3 × 8
6	24 ÷ 3	14	18 ÷ 3	22	30 ÷ 3
7	4 × 3	15	3 × 7		
8	21 ÷ 3	16	27 ÷ 3		

Mark the answers and correct any mistakes in full.

B Write the answers only.

1	(3 × 3) + 1	11	(4 × 3) + 2
2	(7 × 3) + 2	12	(0 × 3) + 2
3	(0 × 3) + 1	13	(5 × 3) + 1
4	(5 × 3) + 2	14	(9 × 3) + 1
5	(10 × 3) + 2	15	(8 × 3) + 2
6	(2 × 3) + 2	16	(10 × 3) + 1
7	(6 × 3) + 1	17	(3 × 3) + 2
8	(8 × 3) + 1	18	(7 × 3) + 1
9	(1 × 3) + 2	19	(6 × 3) + 2
10	(9 × 3) + 2	20	(4 × 3) + 1

C

Tim   Alan   John

There are 7 biscuits which are shared equally among Tim, Alan and John.

1 How many biscuits does each have?

2 How many biscuits are left over?

This can be written in two ways:

$$7 ÷ 3 = 2 \text{ rem. } 1 \quad \text{or} \quad 3)\overline{7} \ ^{2 \text{ rem. } 1.}$$

3 If there had been 8 biscuits, how many each and how many left over?
Write and complete:

$$8 ÷ 3 = ☐ \text{ rem. } ☐ \qquad 3)\overline{8} \ ^{☐ \text{ rem. } ☐.}$$

Write and complete:

4 10 ÷ 3 = ☐ rem. ☐

5 31 ÷ 3 = ☐ rem. ☐

6 1 ÷ 3 = ☐ rem. ☐.

Write the answers only.

7	5 ÷ 3	12	17 ÷ 3
8	29 ÷ 3	13	25 ÷ 3
9	16 ÷ 3	14	23 ÷ 3
10	26 ÷ 3	15	13 ÷ 3
11	19 ÷ 3	16	11 ÷ 3

D

1 From a packet of 25 stamps, how many girls can each have 3 stamps?
How many stamps are left?

2 How many 3p oranges can be bought for a **TWENTY**?
How many pennies are left?

3 How many pieces each 3 cm long can be cut from a length of 32 cm?
How many cm remain?

4 Mother paid for 7 cakes each costing 3p.
If she had 2p left, how much had she at first?

Counting money to £1   change

A Susan, Ann and Philip sort the coins
in their money-boxes.

	50p	20p	10p	5p	2p	1p
Susan	1		1	1	2	4
Ann		2	2	4	3	4
Philip	1	1	1		5	1

Find the total value of the coins in
1 Susan's box
2 Ann's box
3 Philip's box.
4 How much more must each child save
to have £1?
5 How much more has Philip than Ann?
6 How much less has Susan than Philip?

B Mary buys a present for Mother costing 14p.
She gives the shopkeeper a TWENTY.
When the shopkeeper gives Mary her change,
he starts with the price of the present.

He says /14p\ and 1p makes 15p,

and a FIVE makes 20p.

1 How many coins does she receive?
2 How much change?
3 This picture tells the same story. Draw the
two coins given as change and write the value
of each of them. Find the total change.
4 Give this change in another way using
different coins.

coins given	price	change given
20	/14p\	◯ ◯

For each picture story find   a the coins given in change   b the total change.

5

coins given	price	change given
10 **10**	/13p\	◯ ◯

6

coins given	price	change given
20 **5**	/21p\	◯ ◯

7

coins given	price	change given
50	/28p\	◯ ◯

8

coins given	price	change given
50	/34p\	◯ ◯ ◯

9

money given	price	change given
£1	/66p\	◯ ◯ ◯ ◯

10

money given	price	change given
£1	/73p\	◯ ◯ ◯

Counting money to £1

A A boy bought this toy 'Dinky' car. He gave the shopkeeper these coins to pay for it: 1 FIFTY and 4 FIVES.

1 How many coins did he give the shopkeeper?

2 How much change did he receive?

3 He could have paid the exact amount with a smaller number of coins. Name them.

4 Write the coins using the least number which will pay for toys costing   a 45p   b 75p.

Dinky car   67p

Draw this table and fill in the least number of coins required to make the total.

	total	50p	20p	10p	5p	2p	1p
5	33p						
6	61p						
7	58p						
8	47p						
9	72p						
10	89p						
11	94p						

B

The table shows the number of coins saved by each of the children.

Find the total savings of each child.

	name	50p	20p	10p	5p	2p	1p
1	Tony		1	2	1		1
2	Jill		1	1	2	3	2
3	Peter		3		3		2
4	Jane	1		1	1	1	1
5	Stephen	1	1	1		2	
6	Joan	1		1	4	5	
7	Alan		2	2	1	3	

C

	Find the change from 10p. money spent		Find the change from 20p. money spent		Find the change from 50p. money spent		Find the change from £1. money spent
1	8p	7	15p	13	42p	19	91p
2	6p	8	12p	14	48p	20	85p
3	9p	9	16p	15	35p	21	66p
4	3p	10	9p	16	30p	22	37p
5	1p	11	8p	17	17p	23	24p
6	7p	12	4p	18	12p	24	13p

Measuring capacity

A

1 Get two jugs of different shapes.

2 Fill one of the jugs to the top with water.
Pour the water into the other jug.
Which holds the more?
How do you know?

3 Get another jug of a different shape.
Find out which of the three jugs holds
the most.

B

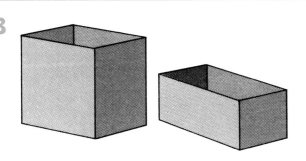

1 Get two boxes of different shapes.

2 Fill one of the boxes with sand.

3 Pour the sand into the other box. Which
holds the more? How do you know?

4 Get another box of a different shape.
Find out which of the three boxes holds
the most.

C

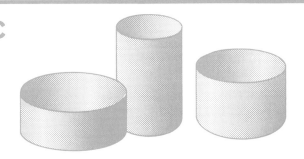

1 Get three tins or jars like those in the
picture. They are similar in shape.
These shapes are called **cylinders.**
Do you think they hold the same amount?
Use water or sand to find out.

2 If they do not hold the same amount find
which box holds the most; the least.

D

1 Get a basin, a large jar, a milk bottle and an empty tin.

2 Use a teacup to fill each one with water.
Count how many cupfuls each holds. You may
have to use a $\frac{1}{2}$ or $\frac{1}{4}$ cupful.

3 Copy this record chart and write the numbers in the
columns.

4 Do the same again but this time use an egg-cup.

You have been measuring how much these containers
hold. This amount is called the **capacity.**

5 Why are the numbers in each item in column **X**
different from those in column **Y**?

	X teacups	Y egg-cups
basin		
large jug		
milk bottle		
tin		

Measures capacity

A

1ℓ
one litre

½ℓ
half-litre

Most liquids are measured in **litres** (ℓ) or **half-litres** (½ ℓ).

The litre is the standard measure of capacity.

1 You will require a litre and a half-litre measure.

2 Find the mark on the side of each which shows the exact measure.

3 How many times must you fill the half-litre measure with water to make a litre?

Collect a variety of bottles, jars, jugs, cartons, etc.

4 Fill the half-litre measure with water up to the mark.

5 Pour the water carefully into one of the containers.

6 Does the container hold

  a exactly ½ litre   b more than ½ litre
  c less than ½ litre?

How do you know?

7 In the same way, find out which of the other containers hold exactly half-litre, or more or less than half-litre.

Notice that two or more containers may hold the same amount but have different shapes.

B

Collect a variety of large containers, a bucket, a bowl, a small bath, a watering-can, etc.

1 Pour 1 litre of water into each container.

2 Use a stick to find the depth of the water.

3 Now estimate how many litres each container will hold.

4 Copy this record chart and enter the results.

5 Use the litre and half-litre measures to find the capacity of each.

6 Write in the chart whether your estimates were correct, too big or too small.

	estimates litres	measures litres	estimate correct too big too small
bucket			
bowl			
bath			
watering-can			
etc.			

Numbers from pictures   block graphs

A

This is a game about birthday months played by all the children in a class.

Each child born in **January** put a cube in a pile.

Next, the children born in **February** made another pile.

Next again, came the **March** children, and so on through the other months of the year.

1 How many piles would you expect there to be? Why? At the finish the piles of cubes looked like this picture.

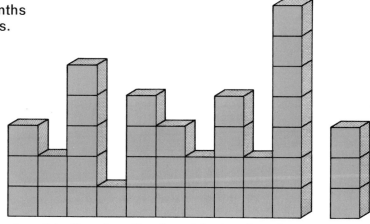

Jan. Feb. Mar. Apr. May June July Aug. Sept. Oct. Nov. Dec.

2 Count the number of cubes in each pile. Draw and fill in this table.

birthday month	Jan.	Feb.	Mar.	Apr.	May	June	July	Aug.	Sept.	Oct.	Nov.	Dec.
number of children												

B

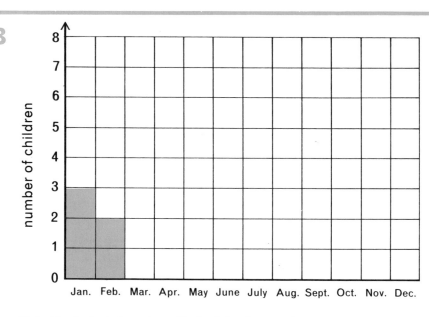

1 Get a piece of squared paper like the one shown.

2 Draw a horizontal line and along it write the months as shown.

3 Draw a vertical line and alongside it mark the number of children.

4 From the table above, fill in 1 square to stand for 1 child. The months of January and February have been done for you.

This kind of picture is called a **block graph.**

5 Find out the birthday months of at least 20 of your friends. Then in the same way draw a block graph to show the numbers.

Numbers from pictures   block graphs

A The picture shows the number of children
in a class who
a walk to school
b come to school on a bus
c come to school in a car
d cycle to school.

1 Draw and fill in this table.

number of children			
walk	**bus**	**car**	**cycle**

2 How many more children walk to school
than
a ride their bicycles   b come by car
c come by bus?

3 There are three times as many children
who _____ than who _____ to school.

4 Find the total number of children
in the class.

5 The table gives a count of how the children
in another class come to school.

walk	**bus**	**car**	**cycle**
18	4	0	7

On squared paper draw a block graph.
First mark the vertical line and the
horizontal spaces as shown in the
example. Let one square stand for one
child.

6 Answer questions **2** and **4** from your graph.

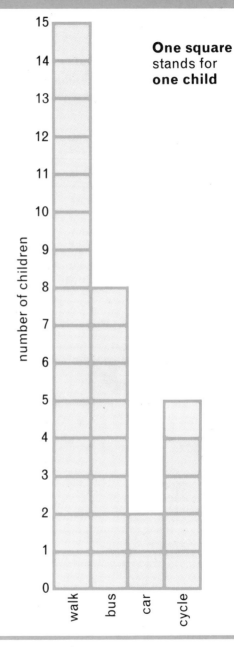

**One square
stands for
one child**

B

1 In your class there are children who have
fair hair, brown hair and black hair.
Count the number of each.
Draw a table and fill in the numbers.

2 On squared paper make a block graph to
show these numbers. First mark the
vertical line and the horizontal spaces.
Let one square stand for one child.

3 Make up some questions which you can
answer from your graph.
e.g.
How many (more, fewer) children
have fair hair than black hair?

4 Think of other block graphs you can
draw, e.g. the number of children who
wear a pullover, a blazer or a T-shirt.

Counting in fours

A

1	2	3	④	5	6	7	⑧	9	10
11	12	13	14	15	16	17	18	19	20
21	22	23	24	25	26	27	28	29	30
31	32	33	34	35	36	37	38	39	40

1 Copy the chart on squared paper.

From 4 count on in **fours** and ring the numbers.

2 Write the ringed numbers.

4, 8, □, □, □, □, □, □, □, 40

0 4 8 12 16 20 24 28 32 36 40

Copy and complete:

3 8, 12, □, □, □, 28, □, □, 40

4 28, 24, □, □, □, 8, □, □

5 3, 7, □, □, □, 23, □, □, □

6 38, 34, □, □, 22, □, □, □, □, □.

B

1 There are 4 wheels on the car.
On 5 cars there are 4+4+4+4+4=□ wheels.
There are 5 sets each of 4 wheels.

> **Remember.** Instead of **adding equal sets** you can **multiply.**

2 How many wheels are there on 5 cars?

Write in full:
5 fours = 5(4) = □
5 multiplied by 4=□
5 times 4=□
5×4=□.

3 How many wheels are there on 3 cars?

Write in full:
4+4+4=□
3 fours = 3(4) = □
3 multiplied by 4=□
3 times 4=□
3×4=□.

Use the number line if you wish.

4 How many wheels are there on 8 cars?
Write: 8 fours = 8(4) = 8×4 = □.

5 How many wheels are there on 0 cars?
Write: 0 fours = 0(4) = 0×4 = □.

6 How many wheels are there on 10 cars?
Write: 10 fours = 10(4) = 10×4 = □.

C

6 sets of 4

4 sets of 6

1 6 fours = 6(4) = 6×4 = □

> 24 = 6×4 = 4×6
>
> 24 is the **product** of 4 and 6.

2 4 sixes = 4(6) = 4×6 = □

Write and complete:

3 20 = 5×4 = 4×□

4 28 = 7×□ = □×7

5 36 = 9(4) = □(9)

6 0 = □(4) = 4(0).

Find the product of

7 6 and 4

8 4 and 1

9 5 and 4

10 4 and 8

11 0 and 4

12 7 and 4

13 4 and 9

14 10 and 4.

Counting in fours

A

1 By counting in **fours** find how many pennies.
Write and complete: $5p \times 4 = \square p$.

2 How many sets of 4 are there in 20?

3 Share 20 pennies equally among 4 girls. How many pennies for each girl?

4 This can be written in two ways. Write and complete:

$$20p \div 4 = \square p \qquad 4\overline{)20p}^{\ \square p}.$$

5 How many FIVES have the same value as 20p?

6 Share 20p equally among 5 boys. How many pennies for each boy?

7 This can be written in two ways. Write and complete:

$$20p \div 5 = \square p \qquad 5\overline{)20p}^{\ \square p}.$$

Write and complete:

8
$24 \div 4 = \square$	$24 \div 6 = \square$

9
$40 \div 4 = \square$	$40 \div 10 = \square$

10
$32 \div 4 = \square$	$32 \div 8 = \square$

B

Write and complete:

1
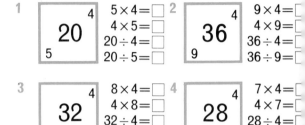

$$\begin{array}{c} 4 \\ 20 \\ 5 \end{array} \quad \begin{array}{l} 5 \times 4 = \square \\ 4 \times 5 = \square \\ 20 \div 4 = \square \\ 20 \div 5 = \square \end{array}$$

2
$$\begin{array}{c} 4 \\ 36 \\ 9 \end{array} \quad \begin{array}{l} 9 \times 4 = \square \\ 4 \times 9 = \square \\ 36 \div 4 = \square \\ 36 \div 9 = \square \end{array}$$

3
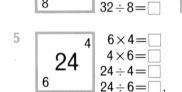

$$\begin{array}{c} 4 \\ 32 \\ 8 \end{array} \quad \begin{array}{l} 8 \times 4 = \square \\ 4 \times 8 = \square \\ 32 \div 4 = \square \\ 32 \div 8 = \square \end{array}$$

4
$$\begin{array}{c} 4 \\ 28 \\ 7 \end{array} \quad \begin{array}{l} 7 \times 4 = \square \\ 4 \times 7 = \square \\ 28 \div 4 = \square \\ 28 \div 7 = \square \end{array}$$

5
$$\begin{array}{c} 4 \\ 24 \\ 6 \end{array} \quad \begin{array}{l} 6 \times 4 = \square \\ 4 \times 6 = \square \\ 24 \div 4 = \square \\ 24 \div 6 = \square \end{array}.$$

6 In the same way, write four facts about 12, 4, 40, 8.

C

1 In the shortest way, find the total of
a $4+4+4+4$
b $4+4+4+4+4+4+4$.

2 12 divided by 4

3 6 times 4

4 How many times can 4 be taken from 20?

5 By how many is the product of 7 and 4 greater than the product of 4 and 6?

6 A cake costs 4p. How many can be bought for 4 FIVES?

7 Which of these numbers will divide exactly by 4?
13, 27, 24, 18, 32

8 Share 36p equally among Joan, Betty, Mary and Jane. How much each?

Write and complete:

9 $\square \times 4 = 4$

10 $4 \times \square = 0$

11 $\square \div 4 = 10$

12 $\square \div 9 = 4$.

Counting in fours

A Copy and complete the **tables of fours**.

Table of fours ×	Table of fours ÷
0 × 4 = ☐	0 ÷ 4 = ☐
☐ × 4 = 4	☐ ÷ 4 = 1
2 × 4 = ☐	8 ÷ ☐ = 2
3 × ☐ = 12	12 ÷ 4 = ☐
4 × 4 = ☐	☐ ÷ 4 = 4
5 × 4 = ☐	20 ÷ ☐ = 5
☐ × 4 = 24	☐ ÷ 4 = 6
7 × ☐ = 28	28 ÷ 4 = ☐
8 × 4 = ☐	☐ ÷ 4 = 8
☐ × 4 = 36	36 ÷ ☐ = 9
10 × 4 = ☐	☐ ÷ 4 = 10

Check both tables and make sure they are correct.

Write the answers only.
Look carefully at the signs × or ÷.

1 3 × 4
2 20 ÷ 4
3 1 × 4
4 16 ÷ 4
5 7 × 4
6 0 ÷ 4
7 5 × 4
8 24 ÷ 4

9 9 × 4
10 40 ÷ 4
11 2 × 4
12 4 ÷ 4
13 8 × 4
14 12 ÷ 4
15 0 × 4
16 32 ÷ 4

17 4 × 4
18 28 ÷ 4
19 10 × 4
20 8 ÷ 4
21 6 × 4
22 36 ÷ 4

Mark the answers and correct any mistakes in full.

B Write the answers only.

1 (3 × 4) + 1
2 (6 × 4) + 1
3 (8 × 4) + 1
4 (9 × 4) + 2
5 (5 × 4) + 2
6 (2 × 4) + 2
7 (0 × 4) + 2
8 (7 × 4) + 2

9 (8 × 4) + 2
10 (1 × 4) + 2
11 (2 × 4) + 3
12 (7 × 4) + 3
13 (0 × 4) + 3
14 (4 × 4) + 3
15 (9 × 4) + 3
16 (6 × 4) + 3

C

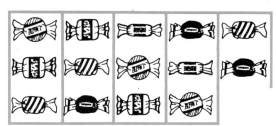

There are 14 sweets which are shared equally among 4 girls.

1 How many sweets does each have?
2 How many sweets are left over?

This can be written in two ways:

$$14 \div 4 = 3 \text{ rem. } 2 \quad \text{or} \quad 4\overline{)14} \overset{3 \text{ rem. } 2.}{}$$

3 If there had been 13 sweets, how many each and how many left over?
Write and complete:

$$13 \div 4 = \square \text{ rem. } \square \qquad 4\overline{)13} \overset{\square \text{ rem. } \square.}{}$$

Write and complete:

4 15 ÷ 4 = ☐ rem. ☐
5 7 ÷ 4 = ☐ rem. ☐
6 18 ÷ 4 = ☐ rem. ☐
7 22 ÷ 4 = ☐ rem. ☐'
8 27 ÷ 4 = ☐ rem. ☐
9 11 ÷ 4 = ☐ rem. ☐.

Write the answers only.
10 35 ÷ 4
11 3 ÷ 4
12 31 ÷ 4
13 37 ÷ 4
14 41 ÷ 4
15 5 ÷ 4

D

1 Share 25 sweets among some children so that each gets 4 sweets.
   a How many children get 4 sweets?
   b How many sweets are left over?

2 Mother has 43p. She buys oranges at 4p each.
   a How many oranges does she buy?
   b How many pennies has she left?

3 32 cm of ribbon is cut into pieces each 4 cm long.
   a How many pieces are cut?
   b How many cm of ribbon remain?

4 How many bags of potatoes each holding 4 kg can be filled from 30 kg?
   How many kg are left?

Whole ones, halves and quarters

A

WHOLE ONE	
$\frac{1}{2}$	$\frac{1}{2}$

$\frac{1}{4}$	$\frac{1}{4}$	$\frac{1}{4}$	$\frac{1}{4}$

Use the diagram to find the answers.

1 Into how many equal parts is a whole one divided to get   a $\frac{1}{2}$ b $\frac{1}{4}$?

2 Copy and fill in the missing figures.

$$1 = \frac{\square}{2} = \frac{\square}{4}$$

3 What part of $\frac{1}{2}$ is $\frac{1}{4}$?

4 How many times is $\frac{1}{2}$ bigger than $\frac{1}{4}$?

5 Mary spent $\frac{1}{4}$ of her money. What part had she left?

6 Three quarters are $\square$ times bigger than one quarter.

7 Susan, Joan, Peter and Tim share a prize equally. What part does each have?

8 Write a sentence telling how you would find $\frac{3}{4}$ of a piece of string.

Write the answers only.

9 $\frac{1}{2}+\frac{1}{2}$ 12 $\frac{1}{4}+\frac{1}{4}$ 15 $\frac{1}{2}-\frac{1}{4}$ 18 $1-\frac{1}{2}$

10 $\frac{1}{2}+\frac{1}{4}$ 13 $\frac{2}{4}+\frac{2}{4}$ 16 $\frac{3}{4}-\frac{1}{4}$ 19 $1-\frac{1}{4}$

11 $\frac{1}{4}+\frac{3}{4}$ 14 $\frac{1}{4}+\frac{1}{2}+\frac{1}{4}$ 17 $\frac{3}{4}-\frac{1}{2}$ 20 $1-\frac{3}{4}$

B

A **part** of a whole one is also called a **fraction** of a whole one.

The two cakes are the same size.

1 Into how many equal slices is each cake cut?

2 What **fraction** of a cake is one slice?

3 What **fraction** of a cake are two slices?

4 What **fraction** of a cake are three slices?

5 If four children each have a slice of one cake, how much of that cake is left?

6 Five slices are more than a whole cake, so another cake is used.
Write and fill in the missing numbers.

$$\text{five quarters} = \frac{5}{\square} = 1\frac{\square}{4}$$

7 If 6 children each eat a slice of cake, how many quarters are eaten?

Write and complete:

$$\text{six quarters} = \frac{6}{4} = 1\frac{\square}{4} = 1\frac{\square}{2}.$$

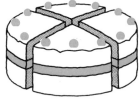

8 Complete these.

$$\text{seven quarters} = \frac{\square}{4} = 1\frac{\square}{4}$$

$$\text{eight quarters} = \frac{\square}{4} = \square$$

Write the answers only.

9 $1+\frac{1}{4}$ 10 $1+\frac{1}{2}$ 11 $1+\frac{3}{4}$ 12 $1+\frac{2}{4}$

13 $2-\frac{1}{4}$ 14 $2-\frac{1}{2}$ 15 $2-\frac{3}{4}$ 16 $2-\frac{2}{4}$

Halves and quarters

A

1. From a sheet of squared paper, cut a strip of 8 squares.
2. Fold the strip into two equal parts. How many squares are there in half the strip? Write and complete: $\frac{1}{2}$ of 8=☐.

3. Fold the strip into quarters. How many squares are there in a quarter of the strip? Write and complete: $\frac{1}{4}$ of 8=☐.
4. How many squares are there in three quarters of the strip? Write and complete: $\frac{3}{4}$ of 8=☐.
5. What fraction of 8 squares is 2 squares?
6. What fraction of 8 squares is 6 squares?

B Put out 12 counters.

1. How many is half of the counters? Write and complete: $\frac{1}{2}$ of 12=☐.
2. How many is a quarter of the counters? Write and complete: $\frac{1}{4}$ of 12=☐.

3. How many is three quarters of the counters? Write and complete: $\frac{3}{4}$ of 12=☐.
4. What fraction of 12 counters is 3 counters?
5. What fraction of 12 counters is 9 counters?

C

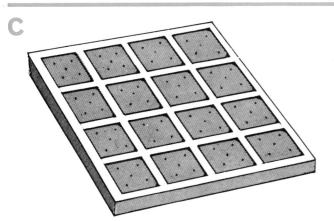

1. How many biscuits are there in the box?
2. George and Mary shared the biscuits equally. How many biscuits did each have? Write and complete: $\frac{1}{2}$ of 16=☐.
3. If the biscuits were shared equally among Joan, Kate, John and Jack what fraction of the biscuits would each have? How many biscuits would each have? Write and complete: $\frac{1}{4}$ of 16=☐.

What fraction of 16 is
4. 8
5. 4
6. 12?

D Write the answers only.
1. $\frac{1}{2}$ of 4
2. $\frac{1}{4}$ of 4
3. $\frac{3}{4}$ of 4
4. $\frac{1}{2}$ of 20
5. $\frac{1}{4}$ of 20
6. $\frac{3}{4}$ of 20
7. $\frac{1}{2}$ of 6
8. $\frac{1}{2}$ of 14
9. $\frac{1}{2}$ of 18
10. $\frac{1}{4}$ of 12
11. $\frac{3}{4}$ of 16
12. $\frac{3}{4}$ of 8
13. Name a coin which is half the value of
   a. a TWO
   b. a TEN
   c. a TWENTY.

14. Alan had 12 marbles. He lost $\frac{1}{4}$ of them. How many had he left?
15. Susan has 16 sweets. She gives away 4. What fraction of her sweets has she left?
16. Eggs are sold by the dozen. 1 dozen is 12 eggs. How many eggs for
   a. $\frac{1}{2}$ dozen
   b. $\frac{1}{4}$ dozen
   c. $\frac{3}{4}$ dozen?

Right angles

A

You see from the drawings above that when a vertical line meets a horizontal line, **a square corner** or **right angle** is made.

How many right angles can you count

1   in the framed picture
2   in the drawing of part of a building?
3   Make a list of 6 things in the class-room which contain right angles.
    Count the right angles in each.

B   Making a right-angle measure

To draw and test right angles you will need a measure. Here are two ways of making one.

1   Get from your teacher a square sheet of thin cardboard. Cut or tear off one corner and write on it **right angle.** Keep it in a safe place.

2   Get a large round tin lid. Draw round the lid on a piece of stiff paper or card. Cut out the shape. It is called a **circle**. Fold the circle twice, as shown, and write on it **right angle**.

3   Fit one right angle you have made over the other. The right angles should fit exactly.

4   Fit a right-angle measure carefully into each of the angles below. Test if each one is a right angle.

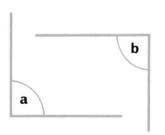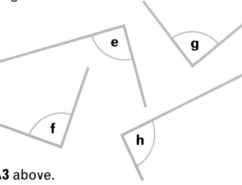

5   With a measure, test the right angles you found in **A3** above.

Right angles

A

1 Draw this table.

right angles	
greater than right angles	a
less than right angles	

2 Test each of the angles using the right-angle measure. Write its letter in the correct place in the table. Angle **a** has been done for you.

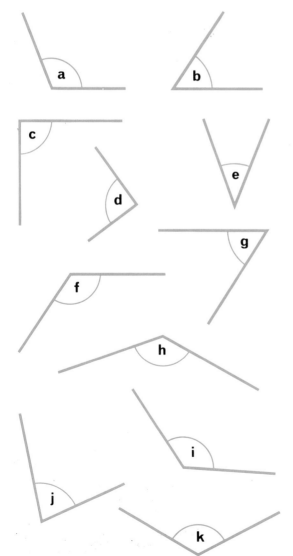

B

1 Draw this table.

shape	A	B	C	D	E	F	G
number of right angles							

2 Look at the shapes. Count how many right angles you think there are in each. Write the number in the table.

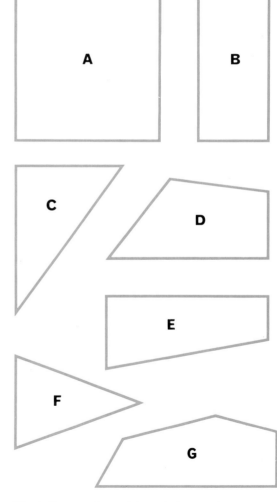

3 Test the angles with a right-angle measure.
Check if the table has been filled in correctly.

Right angles

A

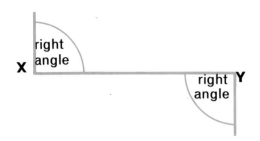

Draw a horizontal line and mark it **XY**.

1 Place the right-angle measure along the line at **X**.
Draw a line from **X** at right angles to **XY**.

2 Now place your right-angle measure at **Y** on the other side of the line.
Draw a line from **Y** at right angles to **XY**.

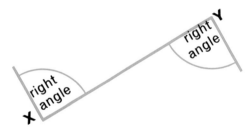

Draw a sloping line and mark it **XY**.

In the same way

3 draw a line from **X** at right angles to **XY**

4 draw a line from **Y** at right angles to **XY** but on the other side.

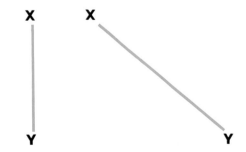

Draw a vertical line and a sloping line. Mark each of them **XY**.

5 From **X** on each line draw a line at right angles to **XY**.

6 From **Y** on each line draw a line at right angles to **XY** but on the other side.

B

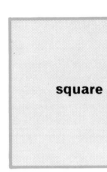

rectangle

square

1 Measure the sides and angles of the rectangle.

2 Draw a rectangle exactly the same size. (Use your ruler and right-angle measure.)

3 Now measure the square and draw one exactly the same size.

4 Carefully cut out both shapes you have drawn.
Place them on those shown.
They should fit exactly.

C

A set square

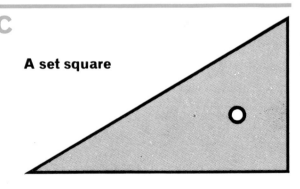

A set square is an instrument used for drawing right angles. It is usually made of plastic.

1 Get a set square. Find the right angle and place your finger on it. Draw some right angles.

2 Draw a horizontal line. Use the set square to draw lines at right angles to it.

3 Draw lines at right angles to
  a a vertical line   b a sloping line.

+ and − number facts   practice tests

Put a strip of plain paper by the side of list **A** and write the answers.

Mark them and correct any mistakes. .

Then go on to list **B** and do the same again.

In the same way work in turn tests **C, D** and **E.**

A		**B**		**C**		**D**		**E**	
1	6+6	1	7+7	1	7+4	1	4+9	1	7+8
2	3+8	2	8+5 ·	2	9+8	2	7+5	2	8+4
3	7+9	3	5+7	3	6+7	3	8+8	3	9+5
4	9+4	4	8+9	4	4+8	4	2+9	4	7+6
5	6+8	5	9+3	5	5+9	5	9+6	5	8+3
6	3+9	6	6+9	6	6+5	6	4+7	6	9+9
7	8+7	7	9+7	7	8+6	7	5+8	7	5+6
8	11−2	8	14−7	8	12−4	8	11−4	8	12−3
9	15−6	9	18−9	9	17−9	9	17−8	9	16−7
10	11−3	10	15−7	10	15−8	10	14−9	10	15−9
11	16−9	11	14−5	11	14−6	11	13−8	11	14−8
12	13−7	12	13−9	12	13−4	12	12−9	12	13−6
13	12−8	13	12−5	13	11−8	13	13−5	13	12−7
14	11−5	14	11−7	14	16−8	14	11−6	14	11−9

Practise these tests again and again.

Play 'Quick Fire' with your partner. Your teacher will tell you what to do.

F

1 Write the missing signs >, < or = in place of ●.
  a 8+7 ● 6+9   b 16−6 ● 3+8
  c 17−9 ● 13−6

2 Which single coin of the nearest value is used to pay
  a 3p   b 8p   c the total of 3p and 6p?
  Find the change in each case.

3 What is the total of
  3p, 9p, 2p and 5p?

4 Find the change from a TWENTY after spending
  a 4p   b 11p.

5 Write and complete:
  a 14p = ☐ TEN and ☐ TWOS
  b 18p = ☐ TEN, ☐ FIVE and ☐ pennies
  c 16p = 1p and ☐ FIVES
  d 19p = 3 pennies, ☐ TWOS and ☐ TEN.

6 There are 18 pages in a book.
  John read 7 of them.
  How many pages were left to read?

7 Joan has 5p and Mary has 12p.
  How much has Mary more than Joan?

8 Mother spent 9p and 5p.
  She received 3 TWOS as change.
  How much did she give the shopkeeper?

9 On a bus there were 8 girls.
  There were 3 more boys than girls.
  How many children were there on the bus?

10 Tim must save 9p more to buy a book costing 15p.
   How much had he at first?

The calendar

A Months in a year

You will need a calendar or diary.
January is the first month in the year.
Here are the other months in a year, not in order.
March, September, April, July, February, June,
August, November, December, May, October.

JANUARY					
Mon.		6	13	20	27
Tues.		7	14	21	28
Wed.	1	8	15	22	29
Thurs.	2	9	16	23	30
Fri.	3	10	17	24	31
Sat.	4	11	18	25	
Sun.	5	12	19	26	

1 Write the months in order. Learn to spell the names.
2 How many months are there in a year?
3 Which month comes before January?
4 How many days are there in January?

month	days in month
Jan.	
Feb.	
Mar.	

5 Make a list of the months using the short way of writing the names as shown in the table.
6 Write in the list the number of days in each month.
7 In how many months are there a 30 days b 31 days?
8 Name the month in which there are neither 30 nor 31 days.
9 How many days are there in that month for the present year?

Ask your teacher about leap year.
10 Is this present year a leap year?
11 When is the next leap year?
12 How many days are there in
   a 1 year   b 1 leap year?
13 How many days in the present year are there in
   a the first 3 months
   b the last 3 months?

14 Here you are told a very old rhyme which gives the number of days in each month. Learn it.

> 30 days have September,
> April, June and November.
> All the rest have 31
> excepting February alone,
> which has 28 days each year
> and 29 each leap year.

B Days and weeks

1 Write and learn to spell the names of the days of the week.
   Monday, Tuesday, Wednesday,
   Thursday, Friday, Saturday, Sunday
The short way of writing the names is
Mon., Tues., Wed., Thurs., Fri., Sat., Sun.

2 How many days are there in 1 week?
3 Monday is the first day of the week.
Which day is the 3rd, the 5th, the 7th or last day of the week?

4 How many days are there between
   a Mon. and Fri.   b Wed. and Sun?
5 If today is Friday which day
   a was yesterday b will be tomorrow?
6 If today is Wednesday, name the day
   a in 2 days' time b in 4 days' time
   c in a week's time.
7 If today is Saturday, name the day which was
   a 3 days earlier b 5 days earlier.

The calendar

A Reading the calendar

Answer these questions from the January calendar on page 62.

1 On which day is
   a 1st January   b 26th Jan.
   c 4th Jan.   d 19th Jan.
   e 8th Jan.   f 29th Jan?

2 On which day is the last day of January?
   Write the date of the next day.

3 How many complete weeks are there in the month?

4 How many
   a Thursdays
   b Sundays are there in the month?

5 Write the date for
   a the second Saturday
   b the third Monday
   c the fourth Thursday
   d the fifth Wednesday.

6 How many days are there between
   a 3rd Jan. and 8th Jan.
   b 16th Jan. and 23rd Jan?

B

1 If the 1st April is on Tuesday, what are the dates of the other Tuesdays in that month?

2 If the 5th June is on Thursday, write the dates of the other Thursdays in that month.

3 If the 3rd Oct. is on Wednesday, write the dates of the other Wednesdays in that month.

   Bank Holidays are days when most shops, offices and factories are closed.

4 Make a list of the English Bank Holidays.
   Find from a calendar or diary the date on which each falls this year.

5 Which of the holidays have the same date each year?

English Bank Holidays

New Year's Day

Good Friday

Easter Monday

May Day

Spring Holiday

Late Summer Holiday

Christmas Day

Boxing Day

C Writing dates

1 Look again at your list of months of the year in order. Name the month which is
   a 3rd in order   b 9th in order
   c 11th in order   d 2nd in order
   e 6th in order   f 7th in order.

   The date — the eighteenth of June, nineteen hundred and seventy-nine — can be written in a short way using figures only.
   Example

day	month	year
eighteenth	June	nineteen seventy-nine
18	6	1979

2 Write these dates using figures only.
   a twenty-third of October, nineteen eighty
   b fifteenth of February, nineteen twenty-one
   c eighth of April, nineteen sixty-four
   d thirtieth of September, nineteen forty

3 Write these dates in full.
   a 5.12.1970   b 19.11.1992
   c 16.1.1939   d 27.5.1951

4 Write your own date of birth
   a in full   b in figures only.

5 Find out the dates of birth of
   a your father or mother   b your friends.
   Write them in figures.

Counting in fives

A

1	2	3	4	(5)	6	7	8	9	(10)
11	12	13	14	15	16	17	18	19	20
21	22	23	24	25	26	27	28	29	30
31	32	33	34	35	36	37	38	39	40
41	42	43	44	45	46	47	48	49	50

1 Copy the chart on squared paper. From 5 count on in **fives** and ring the numbers.

2 Write the ringed numbers.
5, 10, ☐, ☐, ☐, ☐, ☐, ☐, ☐, 50
Notice that all the numbers end in 0 or 5.

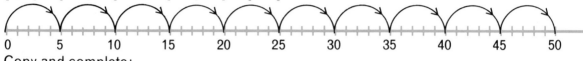

0   5   10   15   20   25   30   35   40   45   50

Copy and complete:

3 10, 15, ☐, ☐, ☐, 35, ☐, ☐, 50

4 45, 40, ☐, ☐, ☐, 20, ☐, ☐, ☐, ☐

5 9, 14, ☐, ☐, 29, ☐, ☐, ☐, 49

6 47, 42, ☐, ☐, 27, ☐, ☐, ☐, 7.

B There are 5 children sitting on the form.

1 On 6 forms there are
5+5+5+5+5+5=☐ children.

There are 6 sets each of 5 children.

> **Remember.** Instead of **adding equal sets** you can **multiply**.

2 How many children are there **on 6 forms**?

Write in full:
6 fives = 6(5) = ☐
6 multiplied by 5=☐
6 times 5=☐
6×5=☐.

3 How many children are there on 9 forms?

Write in full:
5+5+5+5+5+5+5+5+5=☐
9 fives = 9(5) = ☐
9 multiplied by 5 =☐
9 times 5 =☐
9×5=☐.

4 How many children are there on 3 forms?
Write: 3 fives = 3(5) = ☐.

5 How many children are there on 8 forms?
Write: 8 fives = 8(5) = ☐.

C 7 sets of 5

5 sets of 7

1 7 fives = 7(5) = 7×5 = ☐

2 5 sevens = 5(7) = 5×7 = ☐

> 35 = 7×5 = 5×7
>
> 35 is the **product** of 5 and 7.

Write and complete:

3 20 = 4×5 = ☐×4

4 5 = 5×☐ = 1×☐

5 30 = ☐(5) = ☐(6).

Find the product of

6 5 and 8

7 2 and 5

8 5 and 1

9 9 and 5

10 0 and 5

11 5 and 3.

Counting in fives

A

1. By counting in **fives** find how many pennies.
   Write and complete: $8p \times 5 = \square p$.

2. How many sets of 5 are there in 40?

3. Share 40p equally among 5 girls.
   How many pennies for each girl?

4. This can be written in two ways.
   Write and complete:

   $40p \div 5 = \square p$ $5)\overline{40p}^{\,\square p}$.

5. How many FIVES have the same value as 4 TENS?

6. Share 40p equally among 8 boys. How many pennies for each boy?

7. This can be written in two ways.
   Write and complete:

   $40p \div 8 = \square p$ $8)\overline{40p}^{\,\square p}$.

   Write and complete:

8. $15 \div 3 = \square$ $15 \div 5 = \square$

9. $35 \div 7 = \square$ $35 \div 5 = \square$

10. $50 \div 5 = \square$ $50 \div 10 = \square$.

B

Write and complete:

1.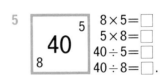
   15 (5, 3)
   $3 \times 5 = \square$
   $5 \times 3 = \square$
   $15 \div 5 = \square$
   $15 \div 3 = \square$

2. 35 (5, 7)
   $7 \times 5 = \square$
   $5 \times 7 = \square$
   $35 \div 5 = \square$
   $35 \div 7 = \square$

3. 30 (5, 6)
   $6 \times 5 = \square$
   $5 \times 6 = \square$
   $30 \div 5 = \square$
   $30 \div 6 = \square$

4. 45 (5, 9)
   $9 \times 5 = \square$
   $5 \times 9 = \square$
   $45 \div 5 = \square$
   $45 \div 9 = \square$

5. 40 (5, 8)
   $8 \times 5 = \square$
   $5 \times 8 = \square$
   $40 \div 5 = \square$
   $40 \div 8 = \square$.

6. In the same way, write four facts about 10, 5, 50, 20.

C

1. In the shortest way, find the total of
   a $5+5+5+5$
   b $5+5+5+5+5+5+5$.

2. Divide 30 by 5.

3. 3 multiplied by 5

4. What number will divide exactly into each of these numbers?
   15, 35, 20, 5, 40

5. How many times can 5 be taken from 35?

6. How many FIVES are equal in value to 25p?

7. Find the difference between
   the product of 7 and 5 and
   the product of 5 and 8.

8. Mary spent 5p a day.
   For how many days would a FIFTY last?

   Write and complete:

9. $5 \times \square = 0$

10. $\square \times 5 = 5$

11. $30 \div \square = 6$

12. $\square \div 9 = 5$.

Counting in fives

A Copy and complete the **tables of fives.**

Table of fives ×	Table of fives ÷
0 × 5 = ☐	0 ÷ 5 = ☐
☐ × 5 = 5	☐ ÷ 5 = 1
2 × 5 = ☐	10 ÷ ☐ = 2
3 × ☐ = 15	15 ÷ 5 = ☐
☐ × 5 = 20	☐ ÷ 5 = 4
5 × 5 = ☐	25 ÷ ☐ = 5
☐ × 5 = 30	☐ ÷ 5 = 6
7 × ☐ = 35	35 ÷ 5 = ☐
8 × 5 = ☐	☐ ÷ 5 = 8
☐ × 5 = 45	45 ÷ ☐ = 9
10 × 5 = ☐	50 ÷ 5 = ☐

Check both tables and make sure they are correct.

Write the answers only.
Look carefully at the signs × or ÷.

1 1 × 5
2 10 ÷ 5
3 4 × 5
4 25 ÷ 5
5 0 × 5
6 40 ÷ 5
7 6 × 5
8 35 ÷ 5

9 3 × 5
10 50 ÷ 5
11 9 × 5
12 0 ÷ 5
13 5 × 5
14 15 ÷ 5
15 2 × 5
16 30 ÷ 5

17 7 × 5
18 20 ÷ 5
19 8 × 5
20 5 ÷ 5
21 10 × 5
22 45 ÷ 5

Mark the answers and correct any mistakes in full.

B Write the answers only.

1 (1 × 5) + 1
2 (6 × 5) + 1
3 (3 × 5) + 1
4 (2 × 5) + 2
5 (7 × 5) + 2
6 (0 × 5) + 2

7 (10 × 5) + 3
8 (4 × 5) + 3
9 (8 × 5) + 3
10 (0 × 5) + 4
11 (5 × 5) + 4
12 (9 × 5) + 4

C

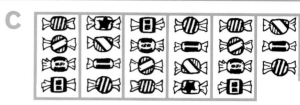

1 There are 23 toffees. Count them. The toffees are shared equally among 5 girls.
2 How many toffees does each have?
3 How many toffees are left over?
This can be written in two ways:

$$23 \div 5 = 4 \text{ rem. } 3 \quad \text{or} \quad 5\overline{)23}^{\,4 \text{ rem. } 3.}$$

4 If there had been 21 toffees, how many each and how many left over?
Write and complete:

$$21 \div 5 = \square \text{ rem. } \square \quad 5\overline{)21}^{\,\square \text{ rem. } \square.}$$

5 If each girl had 4 toffees and there were 2 left over, how many toffees were there?
Write and complete:

6 11 ÷ 5 = ☐ rem. ☐
7 2 ÷ 5 = ☐ rem. ☐
8 27 ÷ 5 = ☐ rem. ☐
9 14 ÷ 5 = ☐ rem. ☐
10 7 ÷ 5 = ☐ rem. ☐
11 37 ÷ 5 = ☐ rem. ☐

Write the answers only.

12 39 ÷ 5
13 18 ÷ 5
14 24 ÷ 5
15 52 ÷ 5
16 4 ÷ 5
17 49 ÷ 5
18 43 ÷ 5
19 33 ÷ 5
20 28 ÷ 5

D

1 a How many children can share 46 pennies if each has 5p?
   b How many pennies are left?

2 A can holds 5 ℓ.
   a How many such cans can be filled from 34 ℓ?
   b How many litres are left over?

3 54 cm of wire is cut into pieces each 5 cm long.
   a How many pieces are cut?
   b How many cm remain?

4 a How many FIVES are given for 39 pennies?
   b How many pennies are left over?

3-D shapes

A Get a large wooden cube like the one shown in the picture.

1 The cube has a number of faces, one is named and coloured in the picture.

Count all the faces. Remember to count the top and bottom.

Write and complete:

the cube has ☐ faces.

2 It has a number of edges, count them. Write and complete:

the cube has ☐ edges.

3 How many of the edges are
a vertical   b horizontal?

4 Count the number of corners on the cube. Write and complete:

the cube has ☐ corners.

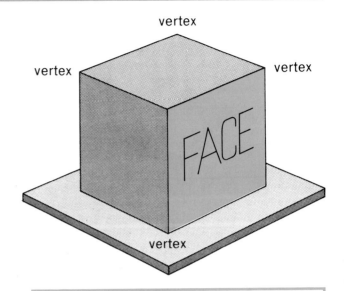

A corner on a cube is called a **vertex**.
More than one corner are called **vertices**.

B Place the cube on a sheet of paper and carefully draw round the edge of the bottom face.
Cut out the shape you have drawn.

1 Fit this shape in turn on each of the other faces.
Write what you discover about the faces.

2 Get some more cubes, both bigger and smaller.

Do the same again for each cube. Write what you discover about the faces.

The shape of the faces on each cube has a special name. It is called a **square**.

3 How many sides has each square you have cut out?

4 Measure the sides of each square. Write what you find out.

5 Look at the corners of each square. How many are there?

6 Fit the right-angle measure into each corner.

What do you find out about each corner or angle?

C

1 You use dice to play many games, for example: ludo, snakes and ladders.

What shape are dice?

2 Make a **Book of Shapes**.

Collect drawings and pictures of things which are **cubes** and put them in your book.

3-D shapes

A

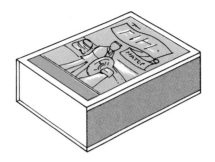

Get a matchbox.
Collect other boxes of similar shape
for example   a pencil-box   a shoe-box
                     a toy car box.

1 Look at these boxes. Write how you know
they are not cubes.

2 Count the number of faces on each box.
Remember to count the top and the
bottom.

3 Count the vertices (corners) on each box.

4 Count a   the vertical edges
        b   the horizontal edges on each
            box.

B

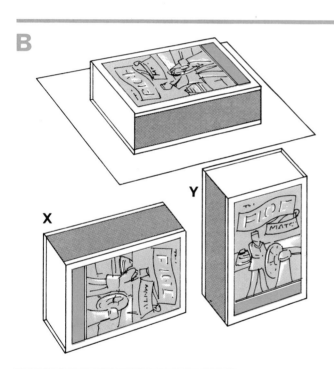

X

Y

1 Place the matchbox on a sheet of paper
in the position shown. Carefully draw
round the edge of the bottom.

2 Cut out the shape you have drawn.

3 Find the other face which this shape fits.
Give this shape a name.

4 Now do exactly the same again having
placed the matchbox as in drawing **X**.

5 Now do exactly the same again having
placed the matchbox as in drawing **Y**.

6 What have you discovered?
Write and complete:
The matchbox has ☐ pairs of equal faces.

Is this true for the other boxes you
collected?

C

Look again at the shapes of the faces
you cut out.

These shapes have a special name. Each
is called a **rectangle**.

1 How many sides has the rectangle?
2 How many corners?
3 Measure the corners with a right-angle
measure. What do you find out about
each corner or angle?

D

Make a collection of drawings and pictures
of things which are like these boxes in
shape. Put them in your **Book of Shapes**.

Think also of big boxes like the living-room
and class-room.

3-D shapes

A

1 Get some containers which are the same shape as those in the picture.

2 On each container, count
   a the number of faces
   b the number of edges.

3 a Place one of the containers upright on a sheet of paper and draw round the edge of the bottom.
   b Carefully cut out the shape you have drawn. The shape has a special name. It is called a **circle**.
   c Which other part of the container is the same shape and size?

4 In the same way, find out if the top and bottom of each of the other containers are circles of the same size.

5 Take a sheet of writing-paper and fold it round to make a shape like the containers. The shape has neither top nor bottom. It is hollow like a drinking-straw or a piece of water-pipe.
   Shapes likes these containers, drinking-straws and pipes are called **cylinders**.

6 Make a collection of drawings and pictures of things which are cylinders. Put them in your **Book of Shapes**.

B

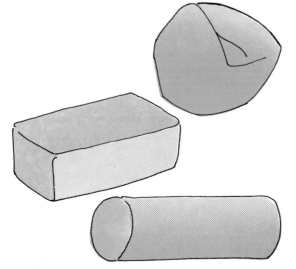

1 Get a large lump of clay which weighs $\frac{1}{2}$ kg.

2 Take the clay between your hands and work it around until it looks like a ball. Weigh the ball of clay.

3 Now beat the clay until it is in the form of a brick.
   Weigh the clay brick.

4 Roll the clay between your hands until it is shaped like a cylinder.
   Weigh the cylinder.

5 Make other shapes with the clay and weigh them each time.

6 What have you discovered about the mass of the lump of clay and the masses of the different clay shapes you made?

Tens and units addition

A

1. 26=2 tens ☐ units
2. 41=☐ tens 1 unit
3. 60=6 tens ☐ units
4. 58=☐ tens 8 units
5. 39=3 tens ☐ units
6. 17=☐ ten 7 units
7. 34p=☐ TENS ☐p
8. 56p=☐ TENS ☐p
9. 68p=☐ TENS ☐p
10. 19p=☐ TEN ☐p
11. 76p=☐ TENS ☐p
12. 80p=☐ TENS ☐p

B

Write the answers only.

	a	b	c		a	b	c
1	11+8	21+8	31+8	2	4+13	4+23	4+43
3	7+12	7+32	7+52	4	12+6	42+6	92+6

Susan has 23 sweets.   23 = 2 tens 3 units
Mary has 14 sweets.   +14 = +1 ten 4 units
How many sweets have they altogether?   3 tens 7 units = 37

5. Write the working in this example and fill in the missing numbers.

Peter has 32 marbles.   32 = ☐ tens ☐ units
Jack has 17 marbles.   +17 = +☐ ten ☐ units
What is the total?   ☐ tens ☐ units = ☐

Write the answers only.

6	35 +24	7	44 +43	8	62 +17	9	12 +76	10	35 +52
11	73p +25p	12	12 cm +84 cm	13	56p +23p	14	60 cm +38 cm	15	28p +51p

C

Write the answers only.

	a	b	c		a	b	c
1	2+18	2+38	2+88	2	13+7	43+7	63+7
3	15+5	45+5	75+5	4	4+16	4+36	4+56

Pat saved 34p.   34p = 3 TENS 4p
Father gave him 46p.   +46p = +4 TENS 6p
How much has he altogether?   7 TENS 10p = 80p

5. Write the working in this example and fill in the missing numbers.

A line measures 52 cm.   52 cm = ☐ tens ☐ units
Another line measures 28 cm.   +28 cm = +☐ tens ☐ units
What is their total length?   ☐ tens ☐ units = ☐ cm

Write the answers only.

6	35p +55p	7	49 +31	8	63 cm +27 cm	9	76 +14	10	48p +32p

Tens and units addition

A Write the answers only.

	a	b	c		a	b	c
1	8+5	8+15	8+25	2	6+7	16+7	36+7
3	9+4	19+4	49+4	4	2+9	42+9	72+9

5 a 3 tens 12 units =☐   b 5 tens 18 units =☐   c 2 tens 13 units =☐

6 a 7 tens 17 units =☐   b 4 tens 11 units =☐   c 6 tens 15 units =☐

A line measures 48 cm.   48 cm   =   4 tens   8 units
Another line measures 37 cm.   +37 cm   =   +3 tens   7 units

What is the total length of the lines?   7 tens 15 units = 8 tens 5 units
                                                             = 85 cm

---

7 Write the working in this example and fill in the missing numbers.

John scores 36 points.   36   =   ☐ tens ☐ units
Joan scores 55 points.   +55   = +☐ tens ☐ units
How many points do they score altogether?   ☐ tens ☐ units = ☐

Write the answers only.

8	26 +27	9	28p +53p	10	75 +19	11	24 cm +38 cm	12	67 +17
13	43p +29p	14	25 cm +66 cm	15	47 +48	16	75p +18p	17	52 +39
18	18 cm +38 cm	19	39p +56p	20	64 +29	21	19 cm +68 cm	22	49 +35

B

1 Add 17p to 30p.

2 24 plus 55

3 What number is 17 more than 28?

4 Find the total of 34 and 37.

5 In a class there were 17 boys and 15 girls.
   How many children altogether?

6 A line 30 cm long was increased by
   16 cm. Find its length.

7 Find and then add the odd numbers.
   27, 15, 18, 24, 9

8 Tim's pocket-money was 35p. It was
   increased by 15p.
   How much does he now receive?

9 Father gave Joan 3 TENS and 4 TWOS.
   Mother gave her 3 FIVES.
   How much money had she then?

price-list		
notepaper	envelopes	ball-pen
28p (per packet)	19p (per packet)	34p

Find the cost of

10 a packet of notepaper and envelopes

11 a ball-pen and a packet of notepaper

12 a packet of envelopes and a ball-pen.

Tens and units subtraction

A Write the answers only.

	a	b	c			a	b	c
1	17−3	27−3	47−3	2		19−5	39−5	79−5
3	15−4	35−4	65−4	4		18−6	48−6	98−6
5	16−5	46−5	86−5	6		14−3	54−3	74−3

Kevin has a book of 36 pages.   **36 = 3 tens 6 units**

He reads 12 pages.   **−12 = −1 ten   2 units**

How many pages are left to read?   **2 tens 4 units = 24**

---

7 Write the working in this example and fill in the missing numbers.

A double-decker bus has 59 passengers.   59 = ☐ tens ☐ units

Downstairs there are 32 passengers.   −32 = −☐ tens ☐ units

How many passengers are there upstairs?   ☐ tens ☐ units = ☐

Write the answers only.

	8	9	10	11	12
	28	47	35	69	74
	−15	−22	−21	−44	−50

	13	14	15	16	17
	58p	99 cm	81p	97p	66 cm
	−33p	−56 cm	−41p	−64p	−26 cm

B Write and complete.

	a	b	c
1	30=2 tens ☐ units	50=4 tens ☐ units	80=7 tens ☐ units
2	40=☐ tens 10 units	60=☐ tens 10 units	90=☐ tens 10 units

Peter had 60p.   **60p = 5 TENS 10p**

He spent 34p.   **−34p = −3 TENS 4p**

How much has he left?   **2 TENS 6p = 26p**

---

3 Write the working in this example and fill in the missing numbers.

Joan has 70p.   70p = ☐ TENS 10p

Jill has 42p.   −42p = −☐ TENS ☐p

How much more has Joan than Jill?   ☐ TENS ☐p = ☐p

Write the answers only.

	4	5	6	7	8
	50	80	40	90	70
	−23	−31	−37	−65	−44

	9	10	11	12	13
	30p	60 cm	80p	70p	90 cm
	−19p	−52 cm	−36p	−53p	−28 cm

Tens and units subtraction

A Write the answers only.

	a	b	c		a	b	c
1	16−9	26−9	56−9	2	17−8	37−8	87−8
3	14−7	34−7	74−7	4	13−5	43−5	63−5

5 a 37=2 tens ☐ units   b 52=4 tens ☐ units   c 75=6 tens ☐ units

6 a 41=☐ tens 11 units   b 64=☐ tens 14 units   c 87=☐ tens 17 units

---

A piece of wood measures 85 cm.   85 cm =   **7 tens 15 units**

Tim cuts off 38 cm.   −38 cm =   **−3 tens   8 units**

How many cm are left?   **4 tens   7 units =   47**

---

7 Write the working in this example and fill in the missing numbers.

A piece of ribbon measures 63 cm.   63 cm =   ☐ tens   13 units

Jill cuts off 27 cm.   −27 cm =   −☐ tens   ☐ units

How many cm are left?   ☐ tens   ☐ units = ☐

Write the answers only.

8	9	10	11	12
44 −19	51 −28	62 −47	63 −34	71 −66

13	14	15	16	17
54p −25p	78 cm −39 cm	83p −56p	95p −67p	62 cm −45 cm

18	19	20	21	22
33p −18p	71 cm −43 cm	87p −19p	62p −13p	94 cm −26 cm

B

1 From 69 take 42.

2 Take 76 from 90.

3 What number is 19 less than 85?

4 How many more than 38 is 90?

5 What is the difference between 50p and 95p?

6 Tim saved 46p and spent 38p on a notebook. How much had he left?

7 In a box were 61 pencils. Tracey gave out 32. How many were left?

8 By how much is 37p less than 50p?

9 From the largest number take the smallest.
27,   52,   76,   28

10 What sum of money must be added to 34p to make 82p?

11 Find the difference between the longest and shortest of these measurements.
18 cm,   40 cm,   64 cm,   26 cm

12 The price of an article was increased from 65p to 71p. Find the increase.

13 Find the difference between the odd numbers.   19,   36,   12,   73,   64

14 Susan saved 60p. How much more must she save to have £1·00?

Shapes   squares

A   This shape is a **square**.

1   How many sides has a square?

2   Measure each side of the square in cm.

3   What is the distance in cm all round the square?

4   How many angles has the square?

5   Use your right-angle measure or a set square to find if the angles are right angles.

B   Shape **N** is a square of different size.

1   Measure the length of each side in cm.

2   What is the distance in cm all round the square?

3   Write and complete:
The square has ☐ angles which are all_____ _____.

Look at page 60, Section **A**. It will remind you how to draw right angles using a measure or a set square.

4   Draw squares **M** and **N** and cut them out carefully.

5   Place square **N** on square **M**. Which square has the bigger space?

Remember what you have learnt about squares.

6   Write and complete:
A square has ☐ sides and ☐ angles. The sides are the _____ length, the angles are _____ _____.

7   Use your ruler and right-angle measure to draw three squares:
a sides 3 cm long   b sides 6 cm long
c sides 10 cm long.
(Look again at page 60.)

8   What is the distance in cm all round square **a**, square **b**, square **c**?

C

1   Get four strips of equal length. Fasten them together to make a square.

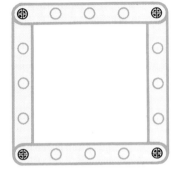

2   Push the square from the top corner and make a different shape.

3   Make a sketch of the new shape. Remember the sides are of equal length.

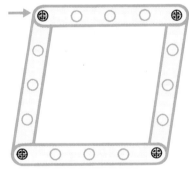

4   Make the square again. Push from the opposite top corner. Make a sketch of the new shape.

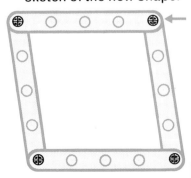

Shapes rectangles

A

1 Look at this shape. Is it a square?
Write a sentence to say how this shape is different from a square.
This shape is called a **rectangle**.

2 Measure in cm the two long sides.
These are **opposite** sides.

3 Measure in cm the two short sides.
These are **opposite** sides.

4 How far is it all round the rectangle?

5 How many corners has the rectangle?

6 Use your measure or a set square to find if the angles are right angles.

B

This is a **rectangle** of different size.

1 Measure in cm
  a the two long sides   b the two short sides.

2 What is the distance in cm all round the rectangle?

3 The rectangle has ☐ angles which
are all _____ _____.

Remember what you have learnt about rectangles.

4 Write and complete:
A rectangle has ☐ sides and ☐ angles.
The opposite sides are _____ in length.
The angles are _____ _____.

5 Use a ruler and a measure or set square to
find out if the following shapes are rectangles.
Then measure and draw each one.
(Look again at page 60.)

a

b

6 Cut out the shapes you have drawn and see if they fit exactly.

C

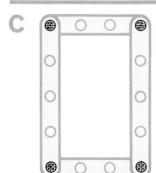 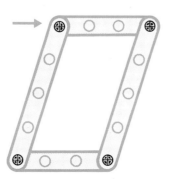

1 Get four strips and fasten them together to make a rectangle.

2 Push the rectangle from the top corner and make a different shape.
Make a sketch of the new shape.

3 Make the rectangle again and push from the opposite top corner.
Make a sketch of the new shape.

Shapes   circles

A

These shapes are called **circles**.
They have been made by drawing round the edge of a 1p coin and a FIVE.

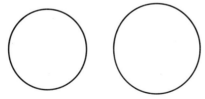

1   On a piece of paper draw circles of these sizes.

2   Draw larger and smaller circles by using other coins.
   Which coins can you **not** use to draw circles?

3   Find other things in the class-room or at home and use them for drawing circles of different sizes, e.g. tin lids, plates, jars, etc.

4   Cut out all the circles you have drawn.

B

Here are some things which move.

1   What helps each of these things to move easily?

2   Can you think why wheels must be in the shape of a circle?

3   Try all the circular things you have collected to see how easily they will roll.

C

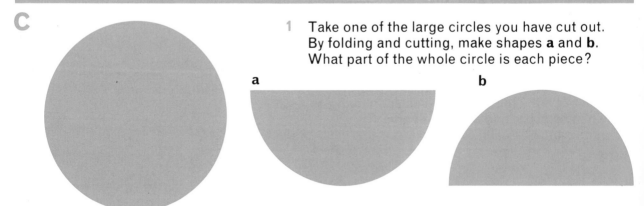

1   Take one of the large circles you have cut out.
   By folding and cutting, make shapes **a** and **b**.
   What part of the whole circle is each piece?

a

b

2   Take another large circle.
   By folding and cutting, make shapes **c**, **d**, **e** and **f**.
   What part of the whole circle is each piece?
   Repeat the exercises with other circles.

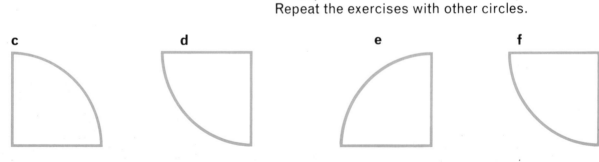

c

d

e

f

Shapes   squares, rectangles, circles

A   You will need a centimetre-ruler and a right-angle measure or set square.

1   Find by measuring
which of these shapes
are squares.

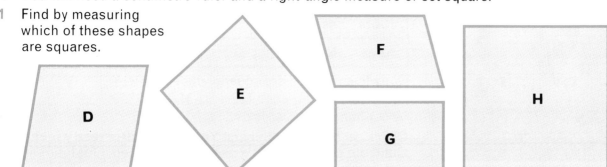

2   Find by measuring which of these shapes are rectangles.

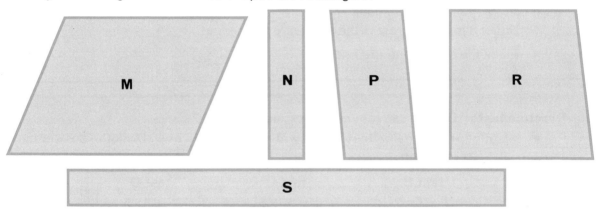

3   Find the distance in cm all round
shape **E**;   shape **F**;   shape **H**;   shape **M**;   shape **N**;   shape **S**.

4   Find the distance in cm all round   a a square of 9 cm side   b a square of 20 cm side.

5   Find the distance in cm all round
a a rectangle 9 cm long and 4 cm wide   b a rectangle 20 cm long and half as wide
c a rectangle 15 cm long and 8 cm wide   d a rectangle 15 cm wide and twice as long.

B

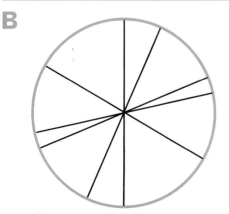

1   Get three round tin lids of different sizes.
2   Draw round each tin lid and cut out the three circles.
3   Take one of the circles and fold it carefully in half.
4   Draw a line with a ruler along the fold mark.
5   Do this again in several places and each time draw
along the fold line, as shown in the picture.
If you have made the folds carefully, all the lines
will cross at one point.
This point is the middle or **centre** of the circle.
6   Take the other circles in turn and find their
centres in the same way.

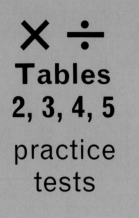

✕ ÷
Tables
2, 3, 4, 5
practice
tests

A

table of		0	1	2	3	4	5	6	7	8	9	10
twos	2s	0	2	4			10			16		
threes	3s	0	3		9			18			27	
fours	4s	0	4			16			28				40
fives	5s	0		10			25			40		

1 Copy this chart on cm squared paper.

2 Fill in the missing numbers in each row by counting in 2s, 3s, 4s and 5s.

3 Check each row of numbers. You have made a **ready reckoner**. Cut it out and stick it on a piece of card. Keep it for future use.

4 These examples show how to use the ready reckoner.

    8 × 5   Place the ruler along the 5s row.
              Under 8 in the top row is the answer. 8 × 5 = ☐

  24 ÷ 4   Place the ruler along the 4s row.
              Above 24 on the top row is the answer. 24 ÷ 4 = ☐

5 2 × 3
6 3 × 4
7 4 × 5
8 8 × 2
9 3 × 5
10 9 ÷ 3
11 10 ÷ 2
12 20 ÷ 4
13 18 ÷ 3
14 45 ÷ 5

B **Practice tests** Do **not** use the ready reckoner.

Put a strip of paper alongside **test A** and write the answers only. Mark the answers.

Then go on to **test B** and so on to **test E**.

	test A		test B		test C		test D		test E
1	4 × 4	1	0 × 2	1	10 × 5	1	6 × 5	1	5 × 8
2	8 × 5	2	5 × 5	2	7 × 2	2	7 × 4	2	3 × 7
3	6 × 4	3	1 × 4	3	9 × 5	3	5 × 3	3	4 × 9
4	4 × 3	4	7 × 3	4	1 × 5	4	7 × 5	4	5 × 6
5	10 × 4	5	2 × 8	5	9 × 2	5	3 × 3	5	4 × 7
6	6 × 3	6	0 × 4	6	10 × 3	6	0 × 5	6	3 × 6
7	5 × 4	7	8 × 3	7	8 × 4	7	10 × 2	7	4 × 8
8	2 × 5	8	9 × 4	8	9 × 3	8	1 × 3	8	5 × 9
9	15 ÷ 5	9	30 ÷ 3	9	24 ÷ 3	9	20 ÷ 5	9	28 ÷ 7
10	0 ÷ 4	10	0 ÷ 5	10	28 ÷ 4	10	30 ÷ 6	10	18 ÷ 6
11	21 ÷ 3	11	12 ÷ 4	11	35 ÷ 5	11	40 ÷ 8	11	30 ÷ 5
12	8 ÷ 2	12	27 ÷ 3	12	12 ÷ 3	12	0 ÷ 3	12	27 ÷ 9
13	24 ÷ 4	13	12 ÷ 2	13	16 ÷ 2	13	4 ÷ 4	13	40 ÷ 5
14	25 ÷ 5	14	16 ÷ 4	14	40 ÷ 4	14	10 ÷ 2	14	35 ÷ 7
15	15 ÷ 3	15	50 ÷ 5	15	5 ÷ 5	15	6 ÷ 3	15	24 ÷ 8
16	32 ÷ 4	16	20 ÷ 2	16	18 ÷ 2	16	36 ÷ 4	16	45 ÷ 9

Mark the answers. Correct any mistakes in full, using the ready reckoner if you wish.

Practise these tests again and again.   Keep a record of your scores.

✕ ÷ Tables 2, 3, 4, 5   practice tests

A Write the answers only.

1 $(7×3)+1$	4 $(1×5)+4$	7 $(6×3)+2$	10 $(7×5)+2$	13 $(6×5)+4$
2 $(4×4)+2$	5 $(9×3)+2$	8 $(0×5)+4$	11 $(8×2)+1$	14 $(7×4)+3$
3 $(8×5)+3$	6 $(9×2)+1$	9 $(6×4)+3$	12 $(5×4)+3$	15 $(0×4)+2$

B Write and complete:

1 $21÷4=\square$ rem. $\square$
2 $36÷5=\square$ rem. $\square$
3 $26÷3=\square$ rem. $\square$
4 $32÷5=\square$ rem. $\square$
5 $19÷4=\square$ rem. $\square$
6 $4÷5=\square$ rem. $\square$
7 $38÷4=\square$ rem. $\square$
8 $7÷4=\square$ rem. $\square$.

Write the answers only.

9 $24÷5$
10 $19÷2$
11 $16÷3$
12 $31÷4$
13 $5÷3$
14 $3÷5$
15 $20÷3$
16 $26÷4$
17 $48÷5$
18 $29÷5$
19 $8÷3$
20 $17÷4$

C Write the answers only.

1 In the shortest way, find the total of
a $3+3+3+3+3$
b $4+4+4+4+4+4+4$.

2 Find the product of
a 7 and 5   b 4 and 9   c 3, 2 and 5.

3 a (5 times 3)+(3 times 3)
b $(4×5)+(5×5)$ c $7(4)+3(4)$

4 a (6 times 4)−(4 times 4)
b $(8×5)−(3×5)$ c $9(3)−7(3)$

5 Which of these numbers will divide by 2 without a remainder?
16, 25, 41, 12, 19

6 Which of these numbers will divide by 5 without a remainder?
23, 40, 37, 25, 52

7 Which of these numbers will divide by both 2 and 3 without a remainder?
12, 15, 18, 21, 26

8 Which of these numbers will divide exactly by 3 and 4?
16, 24, 30, 12, 40

9 How many times can 5 be taken from 45?

10 How many pieces of wire each 5 cm long can be cut from 38 cm?
How many cm are left?

11 7 FIVES are divided equally among 4 boys. How many pennies are left over?

12 Mother has 4p left after paying for 3 ices at 9p each.
How much had she at first?

13 Find the sum of money which is 6p more in value than 9 FIVES.

14 A bag of potatoes contains 4 kg. How many bags can be filled from 30 kg?
How many kg remain?

D Find the missing number in each of the following. Carefully watch the signs.

1 $5×\square=20$
2 $\square×9=45$
3 $\square×5=0$
4 $32=\square×8$
5 $24=3×\square$
6 $35÷\square=7$
7 $\square÷3=9$
8 $21÷\square=3$
9 $4÷\square=1$
10 $\square÷3=0$
11 $3×\square=9×2$
12 $40÷5=4×\square$
13 $3×10=\square+10$
14 $28−\square=5×4$
15 $13+3=\square×4$
16 $2×5=10×\square$

Looking at things from above   plans

A

In this picture Sally is looking at a box. She is looking at it from above.

Ask your teacher for a box with a lid shaped like the one in the picture.

1 Look at the box from above.
   You can only see the **top** of the box.
   How many sides has the top?

2 How many of these sides are of the same length?

3 How many right angles are there?

4 Use a right-angle measure or set square to make a drawing of the top.
   It measures 7 cm long and 4 cm wide.

5 What is the name of the shape of the top?

B

This is a drawing of a box with a lid.
The measurements are given.

1 How long is the box?

2 What is the width of the box?

3 How high is the box?

4 If you looked at the box from above, draw exactly to size what you would see.
   Use a ruler and a measure or set square.

5 If the lid is taken off, the box is empty.
   Which part of the box can you see now?
   Draw what you can see exactly to size.

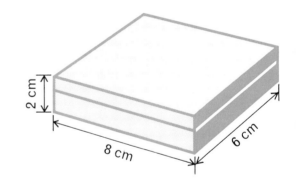

C

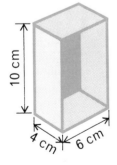

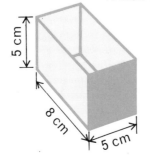

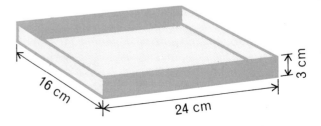

1 Here are pictures of three boxes each without a lid.
   In each case, draw what you would see from above.
   Draw it to the exact size.
   Use a ruler and a measure or set square.

2 Pictures of objects looked at from above are called **plans**.
   Which measurement is never used when drawing a plan?

Looking at things from above   plans

A

1 Ask your teacher for an empty jam jar with a lid.
2 Look at it from above. What shape do you see?
3 Take off the lid. Which part of the jar do you see now?
4 What is its shape? Draw the plan of the jar.
5 Get an empty bucket. Look at it from above.
    You can see both the top and the bottom.
6 Which is bigger, the top or the bottom?
    The plan of the bucket is drawn for you.
    Which part of the bucket is the smaller
    circle?

B Here are some puzzle pictures of things you know.
They have been drawn when looked at from above.
They are plans. Name each of the objects.

Find other objects in the class-room,
e.g. a book, a waste-paper basket, a plant-pot, etc.,
and make pictures of what you see from above them.

Looking at things from above   plans

A

Father

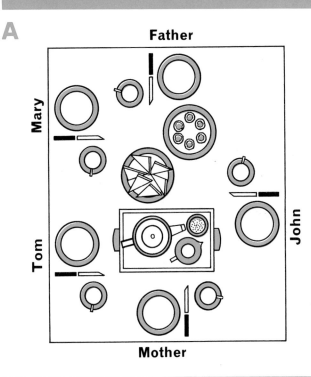

Mary

Tom

John

Mother

The drawing is a plan of the table which has been laid for tea.

1 Which part of the table is shown?

2 Why have no legs been drawn for the table?

3 How many people are going to have tea?

4 There is a plate of cakes and a plate of sandwiches. Write the names of all the other things which are on the table.

5 Count how many there are of each.

6 Who sits on Mary's right?

7 Tom sits on the _____ of Mother.

8 Who sits on the right of John?

9 Who sits opposite to Father?

10 Who sits on the two long sides of the table?

B

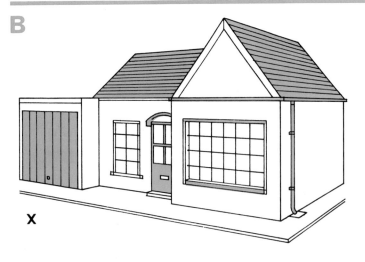

X

This is the plan of the bungalow

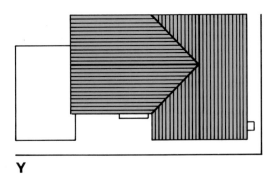

Y

The drawings show two pictures of a bungalow.

Picture **X** shows how the bungalow looks to people passing in the street.

Picture **Y** shows how the bungalow looks from an aircraft.

1 Look at the plan. Make a list of the parts of the bungalow which are shown.

2 Make a list of things which can be seen in the picture of the bungalow but which are not shown on the plan.

3 Draw a plan of
   a a ball   b a lump of sugar
   c a television set.

Looking at things from above plans

A Plan of a bungalow

This is a plan of an empty bungalow. It shows what you can see inside with the roof off.

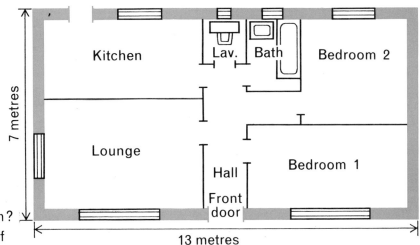

1 How many bedrooms are there?

2 Which bedroom is the larger?

3 Which is the largest room in the bungalow?

4 Which is the smallest room?

5 Name the rooms in order of size, the largest first.

6 How many doors are there? How many windows?

7 How long is the bungalow? What is its width?

8 Where does the first door on the left in the hall lead to?

9 Describe the journey from the front door to bedroom 2.

B Plan of a school

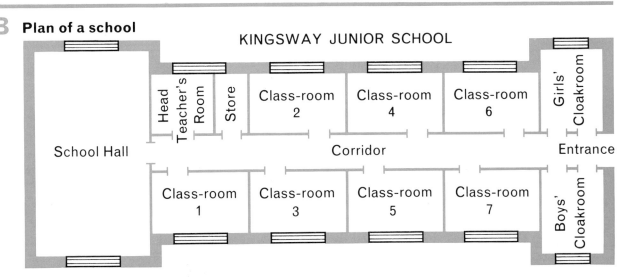

1 Count the number of class-rooms.

2 Which class-room is next to class-room 6?

3 Which is opposite to class-room 5?

4 Which room is the largest space in the school?

5 Write the numbers of the rooms which are the same size.

6 A class-room is the same size as two other rooms together. Which are they?

7 Anne walks along the corridor from the entrance.

Which way does she turn, left or right, for
a class-room 4   b class-room 7?

8 Robin walks in the opposite direction — from the Hall to the entrance.

Which way does he turn, left or right, for
a class-room 5   b class-room 2?

Tens and units multiplication

A

In a box there are 12 eggs.	12	=	1 ten	2 units
There are 3 boxes.	×3			× 3
How many eggs are there altogether?			3 tens	6 units = 36

In the same way find the number of eggs **1** in 2 boxes   **2** in 4 boxes.
Write the answers only to the following.

3	14 ×2	**4**	22p ×3	**5**	34 ×2	**6**	20 cm ×4	**7**	11 kg ×5
8	30 ×3	**9**	43p ×2	**10**	13 ℓ ×3	**11**	40 cm ×2	**12**	20p ×5

B

A box of sweets costs 14p.	14p	=	1 TEN	4p
There are 4 boxes.	× 4			× 4
How much will 4 boxes cost?			4 TENS	16p = 56p

In the same way find the cost of **1** 3 boxes   **2** 5 boxes.
Write the answers only to the following.

3	17p ×2	**4**	13 ×5	**5**	16 cm ×3	**6**	16 kg ×4	**7**	29 ×2
8	15p ×4	**9**	35 cm ×2	**10**	24 ×4	**11**	28p ×3	**12**	18 kg ×5
13	48 m ×2	**14**	27p ×3	**15**	19 ×5	**16**	17p ×4	**17**	36 cm ×2

C

1 Find **a** by adding   **b** by multiplying the total of $23+23+23+23$.
The two answers must be the same.

2 Find the cost of **a** 5 articles at 14p each
b 3 articles at 24p each
c 4 articles at 18p each.

3 A square has sides each measuring 19 cm. What is the distance all round the square?

4 Find the number which is 3 times greater than 27.

5 What is the mass of 5 parcels each of which weighs 17 kg?

6 $\frac{1}{4}$ of the length of a piece of wood is 14 cm. Find the length of the whole piece.

7 A can holds 16 litres of water. How many litres are there in 5 such cans?

8 Mary has 12 FIVES and 15 TWOS. How much money has she altogether?

9 Write and complete: $\frac{1}{2}$ kg × 5 = ☐ kg
18 kg × 5 = ☐ kg.
The total mass of 5 articles each with a mass of $18\frac{1}{2}$ kg is ☐ kg.

10 Find the mass of **a** 4 articles at $11\frac{1}{2}$ kg each
b 3 articles at $23\frac{1}{2}$ kg eac

Tens and units   division

A

4 boys share 48 sweets equally.

How many sweets does each have?

$$4)\overline{48} = 4)\overline{4 \text{ tens } 8 \text{ units}}$$

$$\frac{1 \text{ ten}\quad 2 \text{ units}}{} = 12$$

$$48 \div 4 = 12$$

1 If there were 44 sweets, how many would each boy receive?
Show the working as in the example.

How many sweets would each boy receive if there were
2 84 sweets   3 80 sweets?
Show the working in each case.

Write the answers only.

4 $2)\overline{26}$ 5 $3)\overline{39}$ 6 $2)\overline{28}$ 7 $5)\overline{55}$ 8 $2)\overline{60}$

9 $2)\overline{42}$ 10 $4)\overline{96}$ 11 $3)\overline{63}$ 12 $2)\overline{68}$ 13 $3)\overline{90}$

B

3 girls won a prize of 42p.
They shared it equally.

How much did each girl receive?

$$3)\overline{42p} = 3)\overline{4 \text{ TENS } 2p}$$

$$\frac{1 \text{ TEN}\qquad\qquad 4p}{} = 14p$$

3 TENS ↓

$$\overline{1 \text{ TEN}\quad 2p} = 12p$$

12p

$$42p \div 3 = 14p$$

1 If the prize had been 54p, how much would each girl have received?
Show the working as in the example.

How much would each girl have received if the prize had been
2 75p   3 87p?   Show the working in each case.

Write the answers only.

4 $2)\overline{34}$ 5 $3)\overline{48}$ 6 $4)\overline{56}$ 7 $5)\overline{65}$ 8 $2)\overline{50}$

9 $2)\overline{56p}$ 10 $3)\overline{72}$ 11 $2)\overline{74p}$ 12 $4)\overline{96}$ 13 $2)\overline{58 \text{ cm}}$

14 57 kg ÷ 3   15 64p ÷ 4   16 81 cm ÷ 3   17 76 ÷ 4   18 85p ÷ 5

19 45 ÷ 3   20 98p ÷ 2   21 51 cm ÷ 3   22 70 ÷ 5   23 92 ÷ 4

C

1 Jack has 80p which is 5 times as much as David. How much has David?

2 70 litres of orange squash are poured into 2-litre jars. How many jars are filled?

3 A piece of wood is 52 cm long. What is the length of one quarter of the piece?

4 How many FIVES are given for 95p?

5 84p is paid for some pencils each costing 3p. How many pencils are there?

6 How many parcels each weighing 5 kg are there in a total mass of 75 kg?

Tens and units division

A Division with remainders.

3 boys share 49 foreign stamps.

How many stamps does each have?

How many stamps remain?

$$\begin{array}{r} 1 \text{ ten} \quad 6 \text{ units} = 16 \\ 3\overline{)49} = 3\overline{)4 \text{ tens } 9 \text{ units}} \\ \underline{3 \text{ tens}} \quad \downarrow \\ 1 \text{ ten} \quad 9 \text{ units} = 19 \\ \underline{18} \\ \text{rem. } 1 \end{array}$$

$49 \div 3 = 16 \text{ rem. } 1$

1 If the packet contained 50 stamps, how many would each boy receive and how many would be left over? Show the working as in the example.

How many stamps would each boy receive and how many would remain if the packet contained

2 76 stamps **3** 85 stamps? Show the working in each case.

Write the answers only.

| 4 | $2\overline{)29}$ | 5 | $3\overline{)37}$ | 6 | $4\overline{)45}$ | 7 | $5\overline{)56}$ | 8 | $2\overline{)43}$ |

| 9 | $3\overline{)68p}$ | 10 | $4\overline{)86}$ | 11 | $2\overline{)67 \text{ cm}}$ | 12 | $4\overline{)47}$ | 13 | $5\overline{)59 \text{ kg}}$ |

| 14 | $3\overline{)73p}$ | 15 | $4\overline{)95 \text{ cm}}$ | 16 | $5\overline{)72}$ | 17 | $2\overline{)77 \text{ kg}}$ | 18 | $4\overline{)62}$ |

| 19 | $81 \div 2$ | 20 | $73p \div 4$ | 21 | $41 \div 3$ | 22 | $93 \div 5$ | 23 | $62 \text{ kg} \div 3$ |

| 24 | $79p \div 5$ | 25 | $92 \div 3$ | 26 | $83 \text{ cm} \div 4$ | 27 | $91 \div 2$ | 28 | $54 \ell \div 5$ |

| 29 | $53p \div 3$ | 30 | $79 \div 4$ | 31 | $99 \div 5$ | 32 | $89 \text{ kg} \div 3$ | 33 | $98p \div 4$ |

B Find the cost of 1 article when

		a	b
1	2 articles cost	8p	18p
2	2 articles cost	26p	52p
3	4 articles cost	48p	72p
4	4 articles cost	60p	96p
5	3 articles cost	39p	57p
6	3 articles cost	84p	75p
7	5 articles cost	30p	70p
8	5 articles cost	60p	85p.

9 Find $\frac{1}{2}$ of   a 29 cm   b 35 kg.

10 Find $\frac{1}{4}$ of   a 50 m   b 90 ℓ.

11 Which is the cheaper and by how much per tin
a a pack of 3 tins of fruit costing 57p
or
b a pack of 4 tins costing 64p?

12 A piece of wire is 70 cm long. Divide it into two parts so that one part is 4 times as long as the other.
What is the length of each part?

13 Mother gave £1 to pay for 3 jars of jam. She received 1 TEN as change.
Find the price of the jam per jar.

Shapes and surfaces

A The space in each shape is shown by its coloured surface.
Which shape **S** or **T** covers the greater surface?

1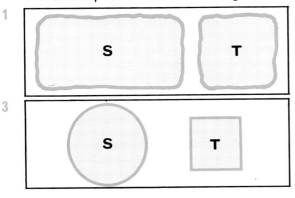

2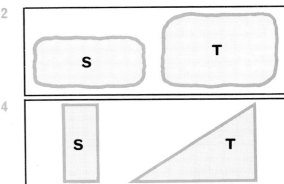

3

4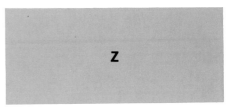

B 1 Which of these rectangles **W, X, Y, Z** has a the greatest surface b the smallest surface?

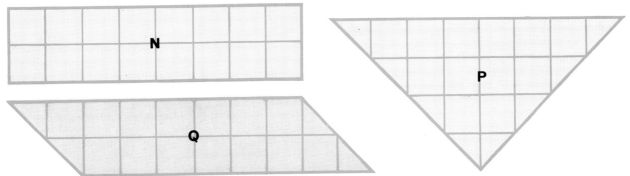

2 Use the letters to put the rectangles in order of size, the smallest first.

C

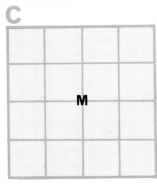

1 On centimetre squared paper draw and then cut out three squares each the same size as **M**.

2 Fold and cut one square in two pieces. Fit the pieces together to make shape **N**. Stick the shape on a piece of paper.

3 Fold and cut another square in two pieces. Fit the pieces together to make shape **P**. Stick this shape on the piece of paper.

4 Cut the other square into three pieces. Fit the pieces together to make shape **Q**. Stick this shape on the piece of paper.

5 What do you know about the surfaces of shapes **M, N, P, Q**?

Shapes and surfaces

A

1 From a sheet of cm squared paper cut out six separate cm squares.

2 Fit together the six squares to make the rectangle **X**.

3 Find the distance all round the rectangle in cm.

4 Make a drawing of the rectangle on squared paper.

Write underneath the distance all round it.

5 Can you fit the six squares together to make a square?

6 The shape **Y** has also been made from the six squares. Find the distance all round it in cm.

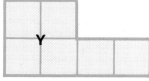

Make a drawing of this shape on squared paper.

Write underneath the distance all round it.

7 Fit together the six squares to make four more different shapes.

Make a drawing of each and write underneath the distance all round it.

8 a All the shapes have the same surface. How do you know?

b What do you find out about the distance all round each shape?

B

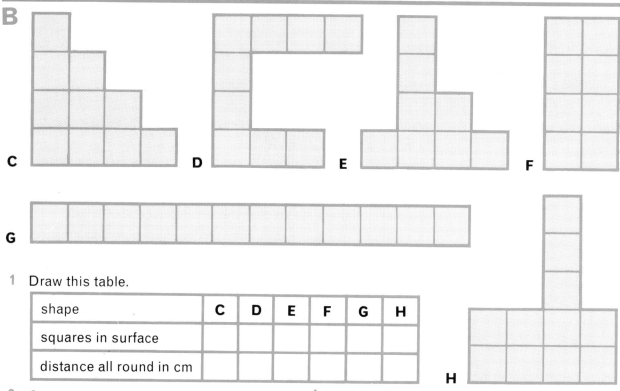

1 Draw this table.

shape	C	D	E	F	G	H
squares in surface						
distance all round in cm						

2 Count the number of squares which cover the surface of each shape. Write the numbers in the table.

3 Find the distance all round each shape. Write the distances in the table.

4 Write the shapes in order of
a amount of surface putting the largest first.
b distance all round putting the largest first.
Use letters only.

5 Compare the orders. What do you discover?

Shapes and surfaces

A

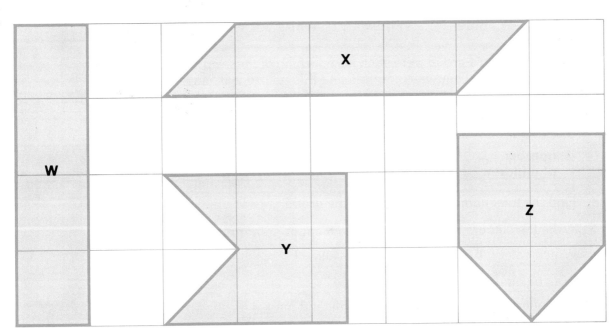

1 How many squares cover shape **W**?
2 In shape **X** first make up the part squares into a whole square.
How many whole squares will cover the surface?
3 In the same way, find how many whole squares cover the surface of shape **Y**, shape **Z**.

B

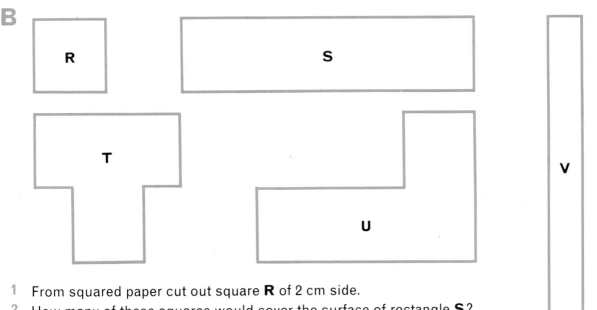

1 From squared paper cut out square **R** of 2 cm side.
2 How many of these squares would cover the surface of rectangle **S**?
3 How many of these squares would cover the surfaces of shapes **T**, **U** and **V**?
4 Which two of the shapes have the same surface?

Test yourself number and money

A

red	blue	yellow	white	black

The children in a group were each asked which of these colours they liked most. They were counted and this record was made.

colour	red	blue	yellow	white	black
number of children	14	18	9	7	2

1 Find the total number of children in the group.

2 Write the colours in order putting the most popular first.

3 Which colour is twice as popular as yellow?

4 Which colour is half as popular as red?

5 On squared paper, draw a block graph, and mark it as shown. Let one square stand for 1 child.

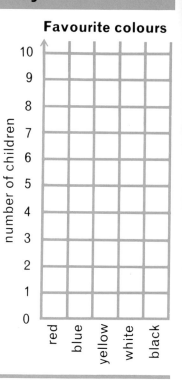

Favourite colours

B The children in Beeches Primary School held a class collection for the Blind.

Weeks	1	2	3
Class 1	24p	17p	32p
Class 2	8p	32p	29p
Class 3	19p	6p	20p

1 How much was collected in
   a the 1st week   b the 2nd week   c the 3rd week?
2 Find the total amount collected by
   a Class 1   b Class 2   c Class 3.
3 Which class collected
   a the most money   b the least money?
4 Find the difference between these two sums of money.
5 How much more must each class collect to bring its total up to £1?

C A ticket for a school concert costs 16p. Children pay half-price.
   How much would be paid by
1 Mr. and Mrs. Jones and their son James   2 Mrs. Smith and her four children?
3 Draw and fill in this ready reckoner.

number of tickets	$\frac{1}{2}$	1	$1\frac{1}{2}$	2	$2\frac{1}{2}$	3	$3\frac{1}{2}$	4	$4\frac{1}{2}$	5	$5\frac{1}{2}$	6
cost	8p	16p										

4 Check your ready reckoner and then use it to find the cost of tickets for
   a 4 adults   b 3 adults and 1 child   c 2 adults and 6 children.
5 How many adults could go to the school concert for   a 48p   b 80p?
6 How many adults could go to the concert with one of the children for   a 40p   b 72p?

Test yourself measures

A

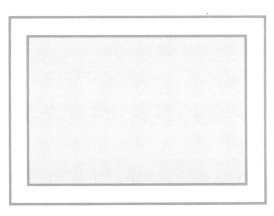

1. Write the names of the two shapes in this drawing.

2. Measure the length and width in centimetres of the larger shape.

3. Find the distance round the shape.

4. How wide is the border?

5. Without measuring, write the length and width of the inner shape.
   Check your answers by measuring.

6. Find the distance round the inner shape.

B

1. Measure in cm the length and width of shape **X**.

   Then draw it to the same size.

   Use your right-angle measure or a set square to draw the angles.

2. Now measure shape **Y** and draw it to the same size.

3. Cut out both the shapes you have drawn and see if they fit exactly over the printed shapes.

4. Find the distance round
   a shape **X**   b shape **Y**.

C

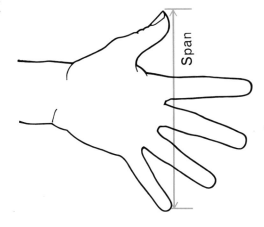

1. Open your fingers as wide as possible and mark your span on a sheet of paper.

2. Measure your span in cm.

3. Find the length in cm of
   a 2 spans   b 3 spans   c 5 spans.

4. a What is the length and width of your desk in spans?

   b Now change the span measures to centimetres.

   c Check your answers by measuring with a ruler.

Test yourself measures

A

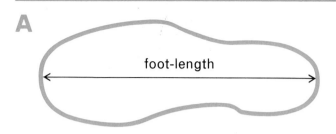

foot-length

1 Take off your shoe and draw round the edge of it as shown.

2 Measure the length of your shoe in centimetres.

3 Find the length in cm of
a 2 foot-lengths b 3 foot-lengths
c 5 foot-lengths.

4 a Measure the width of the door-frame in foot-lengths.
b Change the foot-lengths to centimetres.
c Check your answers by measuring with a ruler.

5 Get a metre stick marked in centimetres. Work with a partner and find by measuring
a the distance you can stride in 2 paces
b the distance you can jump forward.

B

Mr. John Bray kept this record of the number of litres of petrol used by his car each week.

1 During which week did he use the greatest amount of petrol?

2 In which week did he travel the least distance?

3 For how many weeks did he keep the record?

4 Find the number of litres of petrol he used each week.

5 Find the total amount of petrol he used in the four weeks.

6 The dates for the first week were Monday, 3rd May to Sunday, 9th May.
Write the dates of the other weeks.

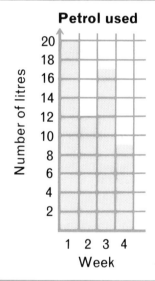

Petrol used

C

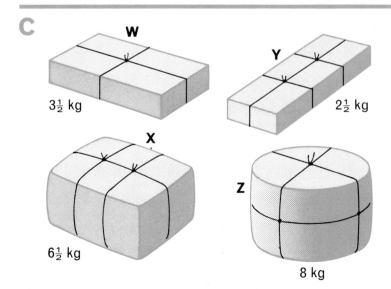

W 3½ kg

Y 2½ kg

X 6½ kg

Z 8 kg

1 Write the mass of each parcel in order putting the heaviest first.

2 Find the total mass of all the parcels.

3 By how many kilograms is
a W heavier than Y
b X heavier or lighter than Z?

4 Which two parcels together are lighter than Z?

Test yourself telling the time, the calendar

A

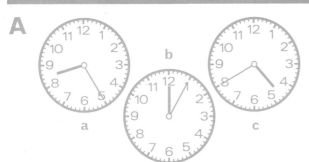

1 Write in figures and in words the time shown on clocks **a**, **b** and **c**.

What is the correct time if
2 clock **a** is ten minutes fast
3 clock **c** is $\frac{1}{4}$ hour slow
4 clock **b** is 5 minutes fast?

Write these times in figures. Use a.m. or p.m.

5 Two hours after 11 o'clock in the morning

6 Three hours before 1 o'clock in the afternoon

7 20 minutes after a quarter to twelve in the morning

8 20 minutes before half-past eight in the evening

Write these times, using words.

9 5.20 a.m.   10 9.35 a.m.

11 4.50 p.m.   12 12.55 p.m.

B

3.30 p.m.	8.30 a.m.	3.30 a.m.
8.00 p.m.	12.30 p.m.	7.45 a.m.

1 At which of these times does Mary
a get up in the morning   b go to school
c have her lunch   d go home from school
e go to bed?

2 There is a time which you have not chosen. What would Mary be doing then?

3 Jack was $\frac{1}{4}$ hour late for school.
If school begins at 10 minutes to 2, at what time did he arrive?

4 Tom leaves school at 10 minutes to 4 and gets home at $\frac{1}{4}$ past 4.
How many minutes does it take him?

5 Bill misses the 11.30 a.m. bus and has to wait 25 minutes for the next one.
At what time does the next bus go?

6 Mother bakes a cake for 50 minutes.
She puts it in the oven at 3.10 p.m.
At what time does she take it out?

7 Joan goes to bed at 8 p.m. and gets up 11 hours later.
At what time does she get up?

C

1 Which is a the fifth month
          b the ninth month of the year?

2 Joan's date of birth is 15.11.1971.
Write this in full.

3 Tom is 5 years older than Joan.
In what year was he born?

4 What is the date of Christmas Day?

JULY					
Mon.		5	12	19	26
Tues.		6	13	20	27
Wed.		7	14	21	28
Thurs.	1	8	15	22	29
Fri.	2	9	16	23	30
Sat.	3	10	17	24	31
Sun.	4	11	18	25	

5 From this calendar write:

a how many days there are in July

b the dates of all the Thursdays in July

c the date of the first Saturday in July

d the number of Sundays in July

e the day school closes for a holiday on 27th July

f what day is   the third of August,

                the 29th June.

Test yourself
lines, edges, right angles and shapes

A In this picture of a building count the number of

1 horizontal lines
2 vertical edges
3 sloping lines.

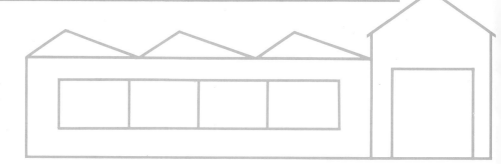

B

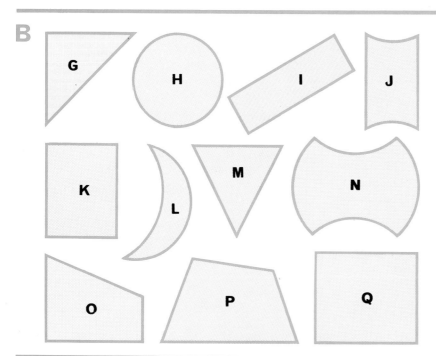

Which of the shapes have

1 straight sides only
2 curved sides only
3 straight and curved sides
4 4 sides
5 3 sides
6 2 sides
7 1 side?

In which shapes are there

8 4 right angles
9 2 right angles only
10 1 right angle only?

C Find by measuring which of these shapes are

1 squares   2 rectangles   3 circles.

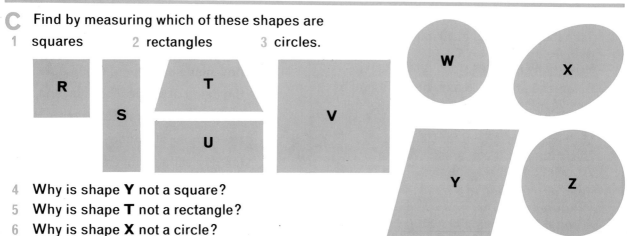

4 Why is shape **Y** not a square?
5 Why is shape **T** not a rectangle?
6 Why is shape **X** not a circle?

Test yourself   four rules

Work Section **A**. Mark the answers and correct any mistakes.
Then do the same with each of the Sections **B**, **C** and **D** in turn.
Write the answers only.

A
1. $3+6$
2. $0+8$
3. $4+13$
4. $12+5$
5. $7+11$
6. $9+7$
7. $8+5$
8. $6+7$
9. $13+8$
10. $7+15$
11. $19+9$
12. $18+7$
13. $20+60$
14. $40+30$
15. $10+80$
16. $39+50$
17. $76+20$
18. $40+57$

B

1.
```
  12
  24
+ 31
```
2.
```
  3p
 16p
+40p
```
3.
```
 18 ℓ
 30 ℓ
+40 ℓ
```
4.
```
  35
   3
+ 61
```

C

1.
```
  35
+ 25
```
2.
```
 18 kg
+52 kg
```
3.
```
 43 m
+27 m
```
4.
```
 54p
+36p
```

5.
```
  13
   4
+ 23
```
6.
```
 32p
 13p
+25p
```
7.
```
 40
 18
+42
```
8.
```
  6 min
 11 min
+33 min
```

D

1.
```
  19
+ 54
```
2.
```
 23 cm
+48 cm
```
3.
```
 87p
+ 8p
```
4.
```
 64 m
+29 m
```

5.
```
 16p
 13p
+ 8p
```
6.
```
 27
 22
+26
```
7.
```
 45 kg
 15 kg
+19 kg
```
8.
```
  7p
 38p
+34p
```

9.
```
  7½ ℓ
 27  ℓ
+14½ ℓ
```
10.
```
 53  kg
 19½ kg
+17½ kg
```
11.
```
 28½ ℓ
 42½ ℓ
+ 9½ ℓ
```
12.
```
 24½ kg
 23½ kg
+33½ kg
```

Work Section **E**. Mark the answers and correct any mistakes.
Then do the same with each of the Sections **F**, **G** and **H** in turn.
Write the answers only.

E
1. $9-2$
2. $7-0$
3. $16-5$
4. $18-3$
5. $20-6$
6. $14-8$
7. $16-9$
8. $13-4$
9. $18-9$
10. $15-7$
11. $23-5$
12. $21-8$
13. $30-10$
14. $50-30$
15. $80-40$
16. $64-50$
17. $96-20$
18. $73-30$

F

1.
```
 57
-14
```
2.
```
 96p
-50p
```
3.
```
 68
- 3
```
4.
```
 98 m
-40 m
```

G

1.
```
 60
- 9
```
2.
```
 50p
-13p
```
3.
```
 80
-37
```
4.
```
 90 ℓ
-81 ℓ
```

5.
```
 40p
-16p
```
6.
```
 70 m
-62 m
```
7.
```
 90 min
-35 min
```
8.
```
 80 kg
-54 kg
```

H

1.
```
 31
-19
```
2.
```
 53p
-15p
```
3.
```
 42
-16
```
4.
```
 75 cm
-28 cm
```

5.
```
 87
-59
```
6.
```
 96 m
-37 m
```
7.
```
 68
-59
```
8.
```
 92 kg
-23 kg
```

9.
```
 31½ ℓ
-  7 ℓ
```
10.
```
 63½ kg
-28  kg
```
11.
```
 40  ℓ
-13½ ℓ
```
12.
```
 95  kg
-65½ kg
```

Show the marked work to your teacher.
If you need more practice turn back again to pages 70—73.

Test yourself   four rules

Multiplication

Work Section **A**. Mark the answers and correct any mistakes.
Then do the same with each of the Sections **B**, **C** and **D** in turn.
Write the answers only.

A
1. 5×1
2. 3×7
3. 0×4
4. 6×4
5. 9×5
6. 4×8
7. 7×5
8. 4×3
9. 8×2
10. 5×6
11. $(6 \times 3) + 2$
12. $(7 \times 4) + 3$
13. $(8 \times 5) + 4$
14. $(0 \times 3) + 2$
15. $(9 \times 4) + 3$
16. $(4 \times 5) + 3$

B
1. 23×2
2. $21p \times 4$
3. 30×3
4. $34p \times 2$

C
1. 35×2
2. $16p \times 5$
3. $15 \text{ cm} \times 4$
4. $18 \text{ kg} \times 5$

D
1. 16×3
2. $27p \times 2$
3. $19 \text{ m} \times 4$
4. 24×3
5. $18p \times 5$
6. $16 \text{ cm} \times 4$
7. 29×3
8. $14 \text{ kg} \times 5$
9. $35\frac{1}{2} \ell \times 2$
10. $24\frac{1}{2} \text{ kg} \times 3$
11. $16\frac{1}{2} \ell \times 5$
12. $28\frac{1}{2} \text{ kg} \times 2$
13. $18\frac{1}{2} \ell \times 4$
14. $13\frac{1}{2} \text{ kg} \times 5$
15. $17\frac{1}{2} \ell \times 3$
16. $20\frac{1}{2} \text{ kg} \times 4$

Division

Work Section **E**. Mark the answers and correct any mistakes.
Then do the same with each of the Sections **F**, **G** and **H** in turn.
Write the answers only.

E
1. $36 \div 4$
2. $27 \div 3$
3. $20 \div 5$
4. $18 \div 2$
5. $17 \div 3$
6. $4 \div 5$
7. $6 \div 4$
8. $26 \div 3$
9. $30 \div 4$
10. $2 \div 3$
11. $26 - (8 \times 3)$
12. $28 - (5 \times 5)$
13. $7 - (1 \times 4)$
14. $48 - (9 \times 5)$
15. $29 - (9 \times 3)$
16. $4 - (0 \times 5)$

F
1. $2\overline{)68}$
2. $3\overline{)90p}$
3. $4\overline{)84 \text{ cm}}$
4. $3\overline{)69}$
5. $3\overline{)42}$
6. $2\overline{)38 \text{ m}}$
7. $4\overline{)56p}$
8. $5\overline{)65}$
9. $64 \div 4$
10. $84p \div 3$
11. $75 \text{ cm} \div 5$
12. $51 \div 3$
13. $5\overline{)95}$
14. $4\overline{)76 \text{ kg}}$
15. $5\overline{)80 \ell}$
16. $4\overline{)92}$

G
1. $3\overline{)62}$
2. $4\overline{)43p}$
3. $5\overline{)54}$
4. $2\overline{)81 \text{ cm}}$
5. $2\overline{)35}$
6. $3\overline{)44 \text{ m}}$
7. $4\overline{)57p}$
8. $5\overline{)66}$
9. $58p \div 3$
10. $98 \div 4$
11. $73 \div 5$
12. $75 \div 4$

Work to a half.

H
1. $2\overline{)61 \ell}$
2. $4\overline{)86 \text{ kg}}$
3. $2\overline{)77 \ell}$
4. $4\overline{)90 \text{ kg}}$
5. $22\frac{1}{2} \text{ m} \div 3$
6. $37\frac{1}{2} \ell \div 5$
7. $76\frac{1}{2} \text{ kg} \div 3$
8. $82\frac{1}{2} \text{ m} \div 5$

Show the marked work to your teacher.
If you need more practice turn back again to pages 84—86.